Pink Skies…Purple Mountains
George VandeWater

Copyright © 2020 George VandeWater

All rights reserved. No part of this book may be reproduced or transmitted in any form or by any means, electronic or mechanical, including photocopying, recording or by any information storage and retrieval system, without permission in writing from the publisher.

Love-LovePublishing—Encinitas, CA
ISBN: 978-1-7334454-4-3
Library of Congress Control Number: 2019917173
Pink Skies...Purple Mountains | George VandeWater.
Available formats: eBook | Paperback distribution

Dedication

My story is dedicated to three special people: my wife, Barbara, who for two-thirds of a century was the major factor in my life, our only daughter, Kathy, and my brother, Fred, all of whom lived far short of their allotted years.

Acknowledgements:

I owe the satisfaction I have enjoyed over the years to not only the events I was able to participate in, but even more so to the friends I have known, some rare characters, some not, and to my family members, past and present who have stood by me. Special thanks to my editor, Malinda Wilson, whose enduring patience is greatly appreciated. Any factual errors herein are mine alone.

Pink Skies...Purple Mountains

Mooney Pipeline Patrol Aircraft

Willcox, Arizona

July 2003

Foreword

If you've not experienced the early morning light of the Southwestern desert through the crystal-clear air so prevalent there at dawn, mark it down as a must-do, high up on your bucket list. Over a period of nearly two decades and 1700 desert crossings as a pipeline patrol pilot between San Diego and El Paso, I've witnessed the morning magic of pink skies contrasted against the deep purple hue of jagged mountains along my flight path. Even on the hottest days, dawn in the high desert is almost cool. Animals are active on the desert floor and birds of prey are beginning to stir, awaiting the thermals needed for soaring flight. The engine in my patrol plane seemed always to run more smoothly in the cool, dry air. Or maybe it was reflecting my own contentment.

My flight career began in 1948 at a speed of Mach 0.2 (about 150 mph) in my dad's North American Navion which, when hard-pressed, could reach that speed. During my Navy career, I occasionally reached speeds of Mach 2.2 (over 1400 mph) hunkered down in the cockpit of my F4 Phantom at 40,000 feet making dense contrails off the southern California coast. In retirement, I returned to the Mach 0.2 regime flying lightplanes and sailplanes, most of which were quite happy at that speed or less. In about a half-century I had come full circle.

During my most active flying years, from 1954 to 2010, I accumulated nearly 20,000 flight hours, over 6000 of them in various military aircraft. Each flight since 1954 is logged in one of my 18 logbooks. I've always preferred flying alone in the cockpit and I seldom used an autopilot, convinced that my flight hours were too precious to waste on a non-feeling electronic device. Besides the F4 Phantom, I have flown numerous fine fighter and attack aircraft, including the F8 Crusader, the FJ-3 (the Navy version of the Air Force F-86 Sabre), along with the F-100 Super Sabre, F9 Cougar, A4 Skyhawk, and my all-time favorite, the F4D (later F6A) Skyray.

Toward the end of my Navy career, I qualified as an instructor in sailplanes and bought an older Mooney lightplane, flying with my wife, Barbara, to nearly every state in the Union. In 1985, at age 52 I retired after 30 years as a naval aviator.

In 1991, after stints as a recruiter for Spartan School of Aeronautics and as a Cadillac salesman (a must if you're a budding psychologist), I began my second aviation career as a pipeline patrol pilot, first as an employee of Sacramento-based Union Flights and finally as an independent contractor to Santa Fe Pacific (later, Kinder-Morgan). I flew my weekly 1100-mile patrols at altitudes as low as 200 feet above the ground in all kinds of weather, experiencing cockpit temperatures from 15 to 115 degrees Fahrenheit. Wearing wool socks and long-john underwear in winter and chewing ice cubes from my cooler in summer, I racked up 12,000 hours of pipeline patrol. I saw dust storms that reached to 10,000 feet, snow, fog, rain, low ceilings, tornadoes, thunderstorm microbursts, eagles diving on ground squirrels, packs of coyotes running down jack rabbits and even a naked woman enjoying her hot weather dip in an irrigation ditch. How many other pilots can claim that?

My story is not of a hard scrabble climb from the city streets. I was raised in a family that had the financial means to dote on their two boys. Fred and I had nearly everything we wanted and did pretty much as we wished although we hardly ran wild. (Wild in the 1940s was hardly wild). Indeed, like most of our friends, we were subject to rules, only some of which could be bent on special occasions. We had horses, motorbikes, and a speedboat to tow water skiers on the Hudson River.

Dad had several airplanes, two airports, and an automobile dealership. We traveled to Cape Cod in summer and south to Florida in winter. Our family owned several large tracts of land, including a mountain retreat with a cabin built alongside a clear, cold stream and we enjoyed our own private airport.

I was a good student, graduating from high school at age 16. Unfortunately, my good junior college grades ceased when I entered engineering school at Rensselaer Polytechnic in Troy, New York. Not conducive to my studies was my new-found girlfriend and future wife, Barbara. I confess my weekends were not devoted to studying the calculus and engineering drawing.

To make matters worse, in June 1953 I received "Greetings" from Uncle Sam scheduling me for a draft physical and, most likely, duty as an infantryman in Korea where a war was still in progress.

My out was to sign up for naval aviation. And why not? I'd flown with my dad and, beginning at age five, I had sailed many hours with my grandfather. Where else could I combine my two budding interests other than in naval aviation? With two years of college completed, I had the required 60 semester hours (not 59 nor 61, but exactly 60) necessary to be eligible for flight training as a Naval Aviation Cadet. Assuming I survived to mid-level rank, the Navy promised to complete my four-year degree at full pay and allowances. Not a bad deal as I saw it and better than slogging through the mud with the Army. Besides, I was already an excellent marksman and knew how to clean a rifle.

I should note that in my story I use actual names, events, and places. Now in my middle eighties, my mind remains crystal-clear in recalling conversations and events, so if any characters I mention are still lively enough to take umbrage, please do so. It will give me a chance to renew old friendships.

Join me now on my journey through three decades of naval aviation flying state-of-the-art aircraft high and fast, followed by nearly two decades of civilian aviation in a very different environment.

Encinitas, California
November 2019

Chapter One
A Cuban Missile Crisis Intercept

Key West, Florida
22 October 1962
1005 Hours

"Echo Lima flight, Boca Chica tower, you're cleared for take-off runway 13. Vector 180, gate to angels 35. Contact Tarpon on button 5."

"Roger tower, 01 rolling," I respond.

My deerskin-gloved left hand eases the stubby, black throttle handle full forward, then outboard to the afterburner detent. A momentary hesitation in thrust, then a muffled explosion behind me as 16,000 pounds of thrust hurls me down runway 13 at Boca Chica Naval Air Station. Seconds later, airborne at 150 knots, nose arcing into the clear, blue Florida sky, my Douglas F4D Skyray, burdened with two 300-gallon external fuel tanks, two AIM-9 Sidewinder missiles, and two 7-shot 2.75-inch rocket pods, still climbs at over 20,000 feet per minute. A brisk right turn to my assigned heading of 180 degrees, my radar scope at the base of my instrument panel glowing, I check in with our Air Force ground control radar site.

"Tarpon, Echo Lima 01 airborne on a 180 vector, gate to angels 35, weapon sweet," I call into my oxygen mask microphone.

"Echo Lima 02 checking in, five-mile trail, weapon sweet," comes the call from my wingman, Leroy "Speedo" Stevenson.

"Roger, 01 flight, in trail come left to 165, continue gate to angels 37. Your bogies 165, 55 miles."

Joe Antel, an Air Force captain and the best air intercept controller at Tarpon, was a good friend. We'd worked many times together in 1961 and 1962 making practice intercepts in calmer times, his voice always steady, comforting, easily recognizable. Joe's control of his fighters was precise, no botched vectors, his ranges to target dead on. If you went into combat, Joe was the guy you'd want calling the shots from the ground.

"01 flight, your bogies have just been designated hostile, I say again, hostile," Joe intones, his voice still rock steady. "Looks like two in trail about one mile apart. They're at 38,000, 450 knots, heading 345…right at us.

"01 roger," I reply, my voice not as steady as Joe's.

Leveling at 37,000, still in afterburner just under the speed of sound, thoughts race through my mind. Is this it? Is the Cuban crisis about to ratchet up to war? If so, my wingman and I will likely fire the shots heard round the world. I peer down at my radar scope. No targets, but there is a strong altitude line on the scope indicating good detection capability. Although the Skyray's radar wasn't the longest-range fighter radar in the fleet, properly tuned it could easily detect a bomber-size target head-on at forty miles.

Suddenly, my scope springs to life…one large radar blip separating into two at 37 miles, right where Joe last called them.

"Joe (I slip into the informal mode we frequently used in practice intercepts), I have two targets 12 o'clock 37 miles."

"Those are your bandits, Ted (Joe too, has shifted to informal). You don't need a visual ID (identification) you are cleared to fire. I say again, you are cleared to fire!" "01 flight roger, cleared to fire, no ID," I respond, my voice betraying a building emotion, an odd tingle running up my backbone.

"02, I'll take the lead bandit, you take the one in trail. Confirm switches hot."

"02 roger, I'm still in five-mile trail, bandits just coming on my scope. Switches hot," replies Speedo, his voice higher pitched than usual.

The blips sliding rapidly down the centerline of my scope, at 24 miles I place my electronic range gate over the lead bandit, squeeze the radar handle trigger and lock on, a large circle instantly blossoming on my scope, the quarter-inch gap indicating a closing rate of 1000 knots, the steering dot just slightly above dead center. Joe has us lined up perfectly. Just a slight nose-up correction to center the dot, squeeze the stick-mounted trigger and at optimum range my weapons system will automatically fire both rocket pods at whatever that radar blip is.

"Joe, I have Judy (meaning I'm taking over the intercept). Confirm we're still cleared to fire."

"01 flight, you are both still cleared to fire. Good luck," Joe calls with just a hint of tension in his voice.

As a former F-86D interceptor pilot, Joe must be feeling the excitement and the stress, maybe even wishing he was in the cockpit in my place. Fighter pilots are like that, even those temporarily relegated to controlling intercepts from a darkened radar control room.

Range now down to 10 miles, closing at 16 miles per minute, I lift the nose slightly to center the steering dot. Odd, but I don't feel fear in the usual sense. After all, a radar blip is hardly intimidating, certainly not like an enemy with his rifle in your face, or bombs going off all around you. But I do feel immense excitement and a building tension, for if this is to be my only chance at war, I'd better get it right. If my weapons system works, if I'm good enough to keep that dot centered at the moment of firing, I'm confident I can down any bomber in the sky.

Hunched over my scope, staring at a shrinking range circle, dot centered, firing trigger mashed against the stick, in just 30 seconds I'll either be a hero or a goat…. But I'm getting ahead of my story. Return with me to the beginning.

F4D over NAS North Island
1958

Chapter Two
The Early Days

The Depression years had been difficult for many families, including mine, to the point that, for the time being, we moved in with my maternal grandparents, George Field Jr. and his Canadian-born wife, Katharine. Grandpa George had done well as a partner in his father's dredging business, had steered clear of the stock market, and lived in a large and historic house in Newburgh, New York with a view of the Hudson River from the expansive front porch.

My parents and I, and later, my younger brother, Alfred Edwin, occupied the entire third floor, sharing with the Fields the ground floor kitchen, dining room, and formal living room. Grandma was a marvelous cook, delighting in providing for the entire family such feasts as roast beef, Yorkshire pudding, and finely diced green beans.

We all got along very well together. Grandpa drove new Cadillacs and sailed his 38-foot R class racing sloop based at the Newburgh Yacht Club where he was elected Commodore. He hunted deer each fall in the Adirondack mountains in upstate New York with his Masonic Lodge brothers and some of Newburgh's most prominent doctors and lawyers. I never recall hearing him complaining of a lack of funds. George Field did what he wanted, when he wanted.

I arrived at a most inconvenient time, just before sunrise on August 18, 1933, my dad wishing he could flee the hospital and get on with his early morning ride on his blooded, former racehorse, Sunflash, mom wishing just to be rid of that pesky lump in her stomach. But then, childbirth was never convenient and there were always more important things to be done in a medium-size town on the west bank of the Hudson River, some 70 miles north of New York City.

As an extended family, we had to work out one small problem involving first names. There were five "Georges" and two "Katharines." My grandfather was George as were my dad and I. To complicate things, my mother's brother, George, and his son,

George, would often visit, so if one called out "George," there was a potential for a stampede.

So, grandpa became "Poppy," and my dad became "Loft," (his middle name). Uncle George and his son became "Bud" and "Tucker," respectively, while I became "Ted." Why? No other reason than it rhymed with my brother's nickname, "Fred." Mom became "Katie" to distinguish her from her mother. None of it made much sense, but it worked nicely. No stampedes.

Mom was born July 3, 1912 in Newburgh, three years before her brother, George Field III, in the same hospital my brother and I were born. Dad, George Loft VandeWater, was born August 12, 1905, in Rahway, New Jersey, the youngest of four boys and one girl. While the VandeWaters were not poor, neither were they wealthy.

My paternal grandfather, Frank, was a perennial inventor and entrepreneur, having contributed to the design and construction of the Correja Speed Runabout (automobile) which in the early 1900s set several hill-climb speed records. He also manufactured paper boxes for the Loft Candy Company. In fact, Grandpa Frank became such close friends with the owner, George Loft, that he named my father after him.

One of my dad's brothers, LeGrand, made a name for himself as Eddie Rickenbacker's director of maintenance in the 94th Aero Squadron in France in World War I. I think LeGrand may have missed an opportunity when he opted to return to his Walden, N.Y. home at the end of the war, rather than to accept Eddie's generous offer to join him at newly formed Eastern Airlines, where Eddie was eventually installed as president.

Dad was a carpenter-builder when he first met my mother in 1930. She had admired him from a schoolhouse window as he labored, shirt off, building a house next to the Newburgh Free Academy. They were married in November 1932. Dad was 28, mom was 21.

Things didn't go smoothly for the newlyweds, dad spending an inordinate amount of time with his racehorse and bouncing from one unproductive business scheme to the next. He was having fun and learning things, he explained. Mom saw it otherwise, being interested less in fun and more in a stable family life. Dad took her criticism under advisement.

Being a pampered only child, I was quite upset upon the arrival of my brother in November 1934. Fred was a quiet, sweet-natured baby, quite the opposite of me, and I remember greatly resenting the fawning attention showered upon him and not me. Being a clever and devious little rascal, I would offer to take Fred for rides in his baby carriage during which I either pinched or bit him, eliciting cries and sobs, and then consoling him with soothing words such as "poor baby honey," convincing onlookers that I was indeed a kind, dutiful older brother and certainly no sadist.

As we grew older, however, my attitude shifted, and Fred and I became the very closest of brothers, always together, sharing common goals and interests. It was a bond unbroken to the very end of his polio-shortened life, three months prior to his 18th birthday.

Country Life

By mid-1943, probably as the result of badgering by Mom, Dad had applied himself in the building business to the point where we could afford to buy our own home, a farmhouse on St. Andrews Road near Walden, N.Y., some ten miles west of Newburgh.

Walden, then a small town of some 3000, is perched on both sides of the Wallkill River, a rather small stream, the flow of which depends upon the season. In the center of town, a large, round clock was mounted on a 15-foot column in front of the Walden Bank, diagonally across from Burton's Diner, an aluminum-clad affair that resembled an Airstream recreation trailer.

Police Chief George Totty, a stump of a man who fancied flared World War I trousers and leather boots to his knees, habitually stood under the clock, right next to a fire hydrant, where he held forth with the locals. One day, as my dad chatted with the Chief, along came a large, male dog, which, mistaking a leather boot for the hydrant, let fly a fire hose stream, causing the Chief to kick vigorously and shout harsh words at the startled pooch.

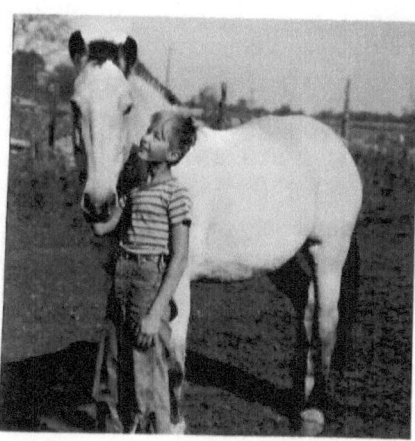

Top

George 1st Row 2nd from Right
Brother, Fred 3rd from Right
Father 2nd Row 1st from Right
Mother 2nd Row 3rd from Right
Minnewaska, New York
July 1939

Lower
George and Daisy
Walden, New York
April 1943

Henceforth, dad noted, the town protector took care to stand well removed from the hydrant, remaining ever on the lookout for stray dogs. Odd, but Totty's successor, Townsend Cocks, who sported standard trousers and low-cut shoes, had no issues with dogs, no matter where he stood.

Our recently acquired farmhouse had suffered significant damage from a recent fire, lowering the price enough to become a two-year project for an experienced carpenter. Dad not only rebuilt the house, but added a garage, chicken coop, and a two-horse stable.

With Dad's racehorse, Sunflash, long gone, our new horses were Daisy, a buckskin mare and Upway Queen Sparkle, a pedigreed chestnut filly from a Vermont horse farm. Fred and I now had horses to ride and to hitch to a buckboard in summer and a sleigh in winter. Country life was good.

From our new home, in the fall of 1945, Fred and I enrolled in a one-room schoolhouse a half mile away. There was one teacher for the twelve students in grades kindergarten through sixth. I was one of three students in the latter grade, along with classmates Leroy Fries and Bruce Wilson, who sat on either side of me in the back of the room.

Other than a water fountain, the school had no plumbing, thus the need for an outhouse which was perched behind the classroom near the playground swing set. Heat was supplied by a large stove in the front of the room, which meant in winter the kindergarten crew roasted while we sixth graders shivered. Between classes, some of us searched for Indian arrowheads in an adjacent cornfield behind an old cemetery whose headstones dated to the early 1700s. The cemetery, and likely a few arrowheads, are still there, as is the schoolhouse which is now a single-family home.

In September 1946, I transferred to the seventh grade at Walden High School, riding a school bus for the seven-mile trip from home. Since the bus made only one run back in the afternoon, I couldn't participate in extracurricular sports. Instead, Fred and I entertained ourselves with our horses and our new motorbikes. In winter, I trapped muskrats, selling their pelts to a local fur buyer for $1.50 each, a large sum in the days when hamburgers were served for 10 cents apiece. I hunted in the fields and woods and fished in a large lake nearby. I had become an excellent marksman with my Savage .22 caliber rifle, keeping the groundhog population in check.

While not much of a hunter or fisherman, Fred excelled as a mechanic and in fixing broken equipment. Together, we modified old cars and even a large hydroplane racing boat which we sawed in half, hoping for more speed. Truth be told, we cut it a bit too short so that with driver and engine the craft had only two inches of freeboard. Thus, unless underway and "on the step," even a small wave would swamp it. We tried it out a few times, got soaked and gave up, opting instead for a 16-foot Larson runabout which, with our 25-horsepower Evinrude outboard, performed nicely while towing water skiers on the Hudson.

In 1946, dad negotiated for a Dodge-Plymouth dealership which he located just outside of Walden in what had been an old icehouse.

Those were the days, right after World War II, when people were eager to buy anything new on wheels. There were no credit card sales. Buyers paid in cash or arranged a bank loan. I remember seeing farmers in bib overalls haul out wads of cash and peel off enough for a Dodge Coronet, a rather poorly built but new and shiny automobile.

Our star salesman was Walt Acosta, a wizened, scruffy-looking little guy. He knew every farmer in Orange County and boasted that if we tacked a Dodge medallion on a shipping-crate he could sell it.

My mother, a beautiful and charming lady, ran our car business as dad was eternally engaged in yet another project. If dad wanted something, he became a dealer for the product. Once the product was in hand, at a discount of course, that was the end of it. No further sales forthcoming and on to the next project.

About that time, dad decided to become a pilot. Kept from becoming an Army Air Corps pilot because of high blood pressure, he nevertheless was determined to fly. First, he leased an airport on the east side of the Hudson River in Duchess County called Freedom Plains. Then, as a Piper dealer with two J-3 Cubs in hand, he hired former Army Air Corps pilots, Captain Don Stroud and Lieutenant "Rocky" Rockwell, to give rides and flight instruction. Don was a towering Maine native who often wrestled with Fred and me but always lost, possibly to ensure continued employment. Rocky, rather slender in build and more reserved, avoided physical contests with two vigorous young farm boys.

As an aside, in the summer of 1955, after I had completed Navy flight training and was on my way to my first duty station, I called on Rocky who was then operating a seaplane base on the Hudson at Newburgh. I re-introduced myself, showed him my new Navy wings and noted that not only was I qualified in propeller aircraft, but was also a jet pilot. Rocky, happy to see me and friendly as ever, seemed impressed.

"Can I fly your Piper Super Cruiser on floats?" I asked.

"Sure," replied Rocky. "Just remember to pull up the water rudder before you add power, get her 'up on the step,' watch out for ferry boats and have fun."

So, without a moment's instruction, and never having flown a float plane, in I climbed aboard with my future wife, Barbara, and away we went, ensuring that the water rudder was up and watching for ferry boats.

Figuring that I had mastered the Navy's flight program (which even he admitted was more difficult than the Army Air Corps syllabus) and remembering I had been around lightplanes for years and had flown extensively with my dad, Rocky indicated that he felt sure I could handle it…which I did with ease over the next few days, taking family and friends for sight-seeing trips…just like I knew what I was doing. All I had to do was to pay for the aviation fuel which was then thirty cents per gallon.

Sadly, or maybe not, according to your view, such a caper would not be possible today with the many regulations which govern civilian aviation, nor are there likely to be such trusting operators as Rocky. Feeling invincible at that stage of my life, I never stopped to consider that I might have wrecked his expensive seaplane. Nor did I consider how I would pay for damages from my monthly pay of $450. Most likely, I'd have become Rocky's indentured servant for many years to come.

Two years later, on my next visit to Newburgh, I tried to find Rocky, but he was gone. A local resident said that he had gone out of business and moved away. I wanted to thank him again for his friendship and his uncommon trust. How I wish that there were more like Rocky in this world.

Chapter Three
Trade-ins and Horseplay

In the family's automobile business, there were always trade-ins which provided great opportunities for me to pick out a new ride. One trade-in of great interest was a 1934 Rolls-Royce sedan with a huge engine and a roll-up window between passengers and driver, especially convenient for carrying on privileged conversations. It boasted top grain leather seats and a beautiful walnut dashboard with two large switches, one for each of the engine's two magnetos. Pointing out that the beast was expensive to operate and maintain, dad quashed the idea.

Next up, and vastly more practical, was a 1932 Chevrolet coupe with a rumble seat, powered by a reasonably-sized engine and halted by mechanical brakes which were nearly impossible to rig so that, under heavy braking, all four tires skidded at the same time. It featured a freewheeling device activated by a huge knob on the dashboard which, when pushed in, disengaged the rear axle from the drivetrain, having much the same effect as merely pushing in the clutch while in gear. We seldom used it. The rumble seat was another matter and a source of continual delight for two lucky people sandwiched in (under a bear or buffalo skin robe in winter) enjoying sunshine and fresh air, although it was not so popular on rainy days. Viewed from behind at night with its interior lights on, the coupe looked like a little lighthouse.

Since Fred and I had numerous new-found friends eager to share our transportation, we decided that we really needed a sedan. Enter a dark-green 1936 Dodge sedan equipped with "suicide" rear doors that swung open backwards, the downside being that should they be opened while underway, an unwary back-seater might well be jerked right out of the car by the slip stream.

While practical, the Dodge lacked the tire-spinning performance we really craved, so our next car was a maroon 1940 Mercury two-door "fastback" sedan with a V-8 engine which indeed met our criteria, even before we "souped" it up. At our first opportunity, we bored out the engine block cylinders, added high-compression cylinder heads, a "three-quarter" racing camshaft, dual carburetors, dual straight-through tailpipes (no mufflers), high ratio Lincoln transmission gears, and lots of chrome engine parts. Our modified car would do 60 in first gear and 90 in second. Fortunately, the roads were not good enough to see what it would top out at in third gear.

How I survived five years driving that car remains a mystery. It was basically unstable due to a transverse leaf spring system which allowed the car to lean heavily in a turn. The brakes, while hydraulic, had limited stopping power. All this, combined with spirited performance, made the car dangerous to a high degree, especially when driven aggressively, which was usually the case. All tricked-out with add-on fender skirts covering the rear wheels, the car was highly noticeable, not only to our friends, but to the New York State Police.

One evening at dinner, mom sternly informed us that two troopers had stopped by our automobile dealership requesting her to relay to "whomever" was driving that marauding Mercury would certainly be caught, whereupon the car would be impounded, and the driver locked up. Expressing shocked disbelief that the troopers could possibly connect a marauding car to her sons, we did promise that we'd mend our driving habits, which we did…for a while. After all, no trooper's Ford could ever catch our Mercury. And they never did.

Ironically, the only speeding ticket I ever got in my Mercury was in January 1954 in a small town in Georgia for driving 35 in a 25-mph zone. The ticketing officer was greatly impressed that I was on my way to Pensacola to do my patriotic duty in the Navy, so much so that he offered to take the five dollars I handed him directly to the local justice of the peace and that there would be no need for me to appear in court. Whatever became of such kindness?

One of our Friday night amusements in Walden, after dining on two ten-cent hamburgers and a five-cent glass of buttermilk at Burton's Diner, was to "flame" Main Street. This we accomplished by turning off the ignition switch while underway and after a few seconds turning it back on which caused the unburned fuel in the exhaust system to ignite with a rather loud boom, accompanied by flames from our dual tailpipes several feet in length. It was quite a crowd-pleaser, never failing to evoke screams of surprise from the strolling young ladies we were trying to impress.

Another fun project was to park just off a roadway traveled on Friday night by urbanites outbound from New York City to the Catskill Mountains. We had rigged a powerful, portable red searchlight to our cigarette lighter and taped it to the car's roof. When a speeding motorist approached, we'd pull out of our hiding place, race up behind the tourist and flash the red light. Convinced they'd been nabbed by the gendarmes, the driver would slow down and pull over, fully expecting a speeding ticket. Whereupon we would roar by, laughing and congratulating ourselves on duping yet another city slicker. It's hard to come up with such fun these days.

Oh, not to forget the midnight golf course thrillers. We'd load up the Mercury with a few deserving local lovelies and drive to a local golf course which featured numerous hills and gullies. Hoping that there would be no after-dark golfers, we'd turn off the headlights and drive off a series of "cliffs" into the dark holes at the bottom. I must say that on a pitch-black night such a maneuver was quite a thrill, even for us boys, to say nothing of the screaming females grasping our arms.

Then too, there was the robust good fun of checking out the local "lovers' lane" haunts on back roads where ardent swains made their play for nubile ladies who agreed to such hanky-panky. We'd sneak up in the dark with headlights off, then light up the suspect car with our searchlight (red lens removed), invariably causing a tumult of activity in the swain's car as he (and she) attempted to reassemble their scattered garments. The most manly of the lovers, when sufficiently garbed, would roar off in pursuit of us. Playing the game, we'd speed down the back roads, headlights off, relying on our good night vision, a little moonlight, and a cloud of dust to make good our escape.

Like every red-blooded teen with a car, we regularly participated in weekend night drag races along Broadway in Newburgh, after the town rolled up its police force for the evening. Our Mercury was never bested, but I was careful to avoid tangling with the rare, highly souped-up roasters which, in the early 1950s, were beginning to filter in from California.

Halloween was particularly fun for us boys. We'd soap up car and house windows and rearrange our neighbors' lawn furniture, some of it ending up on nearby rooftops. My all-time best trick was after dark to throw my lariat around our one-room school's outhouse (first checking for occupants), putting spurs to my quarter horse, Daisy, and dragging it right up to the schoolhouse front door. The school board never figured that one out, speculating that possibly a gust of wind had done the deed. To my everlasting credit, I pulled that caper only once.

A Cabin, a Bulldozer, and Airplanes

By 1948, our car dealership had done so well that my parents bought 20 acres of forestland near Minnewaska in the Shawangunk Mountains, some 20 miles northwest of Walden. With the help of his brother, Harry, dad built a mountain cabin there alongside a brook, ice-cold even in summer, and pure enough to drink. I could reach under rock ledges lining the several pool areas and grab a brook trout with my bare hands, no hook required. There were black bears, white tail deer, and small game everywhere. We had no power or plumbing. An outhouse was perched a hundred feet away, downwind, and lanterns, candles, and a blazing fire sufficed for light at night. We brought in everything we needed during our weekend stays. In the single, large bedroom, mom and dad slept in a double bed and Fred and I occupied bunk beds, one over the other, with canvas strapped to the wooden frame acting as a mattress. One great evening sport was for the brother in the bottom bunk to put his feet up under the top bunk canvas and with a mighty push catapult the top bunk brother out and onto the floor, who usually landed on his feet like a cat.

We operated much like the Peanuts cartoon character, Lucy, who promised to hold the football for Charlie Brown, only to jerk it away just as he tried to kick it.

"No catapulting tonight, Fred," I'd say.

Then, wham, on the floor went poor Fred, taking it all in stride yet plotting revenge for when I had the top bunk. I have nothing but pleasant memories of the days and nights spent at our wonderful mountain retreat, cool in summer, with plenty of snow in winter.

Dad had worked a trade for a medium-sized Allis-Chalmers bulldozer which he brought to the cabin aboard an old Mack flatbed truck propelled by chain-driven rear wheels. Fred and I had a great time driving the dozer, both at the cabin and at our farm. We loved to dig deep holes and refill them, showcasing our skills at handling a rather complicated bunch of levers and foot pedals.

Occasionally, one of the dozer's tracks would pop off, requiring massive efforts with crowbars to get it back in place. Over the years, Fred and I became quite familiar with a broad array of machinery, cars, and airplanes, a great help to me later in life.

In 1949, the family made another purchase: 50 acres of prime land, just outside the Walden city limits. We carved out a dirt airstrip there with our bulldozer and dad brought in an Ercoupe two-place airplane and his new four-place North American Navion (having snared a Navion dealership along the way).

After learning in a Piper J-3 Cub, dad had readily adapted to larger and more sophisticated aircraft, showing great skill in getting each of them in and out of our 1200-foot dirt strip which featured a pronounced hump in the middle. Such a runway configuration made for thrilling takeoffs, with not much speed in hand at the midpoint, but building rapidly on the downhill side to takeoff speed. In hundreds of takeoffs, we never had a problem clearing the power lines at the end of the runway.

Too young to solo, Fred and I delighted in taxiing the Ercoupe up and down the runway when no one was present, raising clouds of dust and stopping just short of reaching takeoff speed. That caper abruptly ended when dad found out from a local farmer that the Ercoupe was often active while he was on away on business trips.

"Stick to four wheels," dad advised us, "until you're old enough to solo."

Alfred Edwin VandeWater
17 November 1934-25 July 1952

During the 1940s and early 1950s, Fred and I lived an idyllic life. We had horses and other farm animals to enjoy, including a pet red fox, and machinery of all types to operate, in the wide-open countryside we so loved.

Tragically, out of the blue, in July 1952 disaster struck our family. Fred contracted the most virulent type of polio and five days later died at the age of seventeen. On Monday I had wrestled with him, on Friday he was dead.

I was absolutely devastated, as was my whole family and our relatives. It was so sudden, so unexpected. Killed in a car accident or plane crash, I could understand. A silent, killer disease I could not. For weeks, despite my grieving parents' best efforts to console me, I withdrew. I took long drives in the countryside in my Mercury, or sat by the brook at our mountain cabin, trying to make sense of what had happened. I could not. I stopped seeing my closest friends. I wanted to be alone, to remember the good times and to make believe it was but a bad dream. It was the worst time in my young life.

A New Friend

Although still feeling the loss of Fred, by late August our longtime friend, Leo Carmody, finally got through to me, insisting that I help him out with a double date he was contemplating. He had met two girls at the Avalon, a local roller-skating rink, who were willing to double date, provided Leo could find a nice guy to go along. I was to be that nice guy.

After a few days of Leo's insistence, I gave in. In his new Oldsmobile Rocket 88 we would take the girls to a drive-in movie, quite the entertainment in the 1950s. Unfortunately, although later proving otherwise, my prospective date, Sandra Lennon, a few days before had overstayed her nightly curfew, so her best friend, Barbara, would substitute.

Barbara Gay Diel, of English and German ancestry, was a Newburgh girl. Her paternal grandfather was a Prussian immigrant who with his wife, Mary, had produced eight boys and one girl. Grandpa Diel kept to himself and after an obligatory "hello" to me went back to reading his German language newspaper.

Barbara's father, Albert, looked much like his father, but was outgoing and a kind and generous man. He belonged to a local Engineers Union and operated a large power shovel on construction projects.

Barbara's mother, Gaynell Stabler Diel, with her Victorian-era morals, was determined to see that Barbara and her younger sister, Bette Jane, grew up properly. Hanky-panky was not for her girls. Not being privy to any of this, I expected Barbara to be the fun type of girl I was used to dating. I found out otherwise…immediately.

My initial view of Barbara was as she appeared from her front porch, walking with Leo while I waited in the car for a proper introduction. She was of medium height, very pretty and well-dressed, with beautiful dark-brown hair, hazel eyes, and a very cute nose. That was the good part. The bad part was that I felt sure I detected an almost haughty "I'm doing you a big favor" attitude. This, indeed, was going to be a different kind of date.

Barbara had previously dated her school's basketball star who, while reasonably charming, was car-less, which meant bus transportation for their dates. I could tell she was impressed with Leo's new car.

Making small talk at the drive-in, I made my patented "first move," casually putting my arm around her shoulders...a major miscalculation causing a verbal eruption that could be heard in the cars parked next to us:

"Get your hands off me!" she shouted. "You fast Walden guys think you can get away with anything. Well, don't try it with me!"

To say I was astonished is an understatement. Taken aback, I tried to plead innocence, but it wasn't going over. Things remained frosty in the back seat throughout the movie, the title of which I don't remember, and during the short ride back to her house. While Leo and his date, Delores, were chatting away having a good time, we were not.

I walked Barbara to her door, or rather I followed her, as she preferred not to walk side-by-side. It was obvious that she didn't care to see a cad like me again, so I didn't ask. Returning to Leo's car baffled, I noted to them both that I doubted we'd be double dating again with Barbara. They did what they could to cheer me up, but I finally told them I'd just as soon return to my Walden girls. At least I understood them and they me. And so went our first date.

Two days later, to my surprise, Leo called informing me that he'd seen Barbara at the roller rink. She told him emphatically that she was not impressed with me and that she'd probably not trust his judgment in the future. At this point, Leo played his trump card. Did Barbara know that my parents had an automobile dealership in Walden? That my dad had two airports, one just outside Walden, where he kept two airplanes? That I lived on a gentleman's farm and had lots of toys, including a speedboat on the Hudson River, and a hot-rod Mercury that was the envy of every teenager in town? That my grandfather was Commodore of the Newburgh Yacht Club where he entertained influential friends and family aboard his yacht?

Barbara hesitated, finally saying she might reconsider and maybe, just maybe, my morals might be fixable. She agreed to have Leo give me her phone number and see where we went from there. Ah, the persuasive power of possessions...but then, one could hardly fault a sweet city girl for wishing to see a glimpse of the good life, could one?

I called the next day and Barbara agreed on another date. I was elated, she was cautious. I told mom the story (well, most of it). She seemed encouraged that I might have finally found a "nice" girl, worthy of the family name (mom could be a little haughty on occasion) and that she'd like to meet her.

The meeting went very well indeed. Dad, who had an eye for the ladies, was most impressed although mom was a little more cautious, wishing to observe how things went before making a final judgment.

Month after month in the fall of 1952 went very well for Barbara and me. We roared about in my Mercury and went boating on the Hudson in the moonlight (me with my arm around her). No more bus transportation for Barbara. As she told her friends, I was showing her the best time she'd ever had. I met her parents who seemed to appreciate my robust sense of humor and her grandfather who probably didn't. It was relayed to me that he thought I drove too fast, my car made too much noise, and besides, I spoke no German. I made a note to steer clear of Prussians in the future, at least grumpy ones who read only German newspapers.

Chapter Four
The Army Was Not For Me

In December 1952, based upon my good grades in high school and at Orange County Community College in Middletown, N.Y., dad thought he saw an opening to finally welcome an engineer into the family. I was to be that engineer.

In January 1953, I entered Rensselaer Polytechnic Institute in Troy, N.Y., very concerned that my Liberal Arts background might not be a good fit for math and science. That concern was well-founded. The calculus baffled me, engineering drawing, where one tried to draw nuts and bolts that looked like nuts and bolts, frustrated me and I was 90 miles north of my girlfriend, Barbara. The only subjects I did well in were chemistry and Naval ROTC.

At the end of May, RPI informed me that if I wished to continue toward an engineering degree, I'd be required to attend a summer session. I was not happy. Nor did the arrival of letter emblazoned with the opening line: "Greetings, you are to report for your Army draft physical not later than 30 June 1953," which meant I'd likely be heading for Korea as an infantryman, hardly something that meshed with my interests in aviation and the sea.

Reporting as ordered for my draft physical, I was amazed at the array of humanity the Army might be considering for active duty. One obese gentleman slipped upon mounting the weigh-in scale, striking his head on the tiled floor where he lay in a state of semi-consciousness. The nearby doctors seemed not to be overly concerned. The poor fellow directly in front of me had only one good arm. His left arm had a set of small fingers where his elbow normally would have been. I was privy to whispered remarks between two doctors, one of whom suggested to his colleague that "the lad might fit in as a one-armed typist." I wasn't sure he was joking.

As I was up next, a doctor stepped close to me, looked me in the eye and asked,

"So, what's wrong with you, son?"

"Nothing, sir," I replied, the impact of which sort of unhinged him.

"Are you telling me there's nothing wrong with you?" he asked again, motioning over another doctor.

"I'm in fine shape, sir," I answered, smiling my biggest smile.

Looking at each other, it was obvious to this medical duo that I had the makings of a mental case. Nobody, but nobody, ever told a draft physical doctor he was in fine shape. They conferred for a few moments, each of them scribbling down a note on their clipboards. Then with a condescending smile, saying something akin to "have a good day," the senior of the two waved me directly to the end of the line where I was told to return next month for further evaluation.

The recurring thought crossing my mind was that I just might be Army material after all, pending a psychiatric exam, of course. Heading home in my Mercury, I resolved that early the next day, right after morning chores mucking out the horse stables, I would rush to my Navy recruiter in downtown Newburgh. The Army was not for me.

Sign Right Here, Farm Boy

Something that morning in July 1953 must have alerted the Navy First Class Petty Officer recruiter that I might not be the sophisticated college sophomore I claimed to be. It might have been my red and black flannel shirt, or my high-top laced up boots with the slight aroma of the horse stalls that I'd mucked out earlier. I hoped he hadn't perceived my desperation to prove to him my qualifications to join the Navy as a Naval Aviation Cadet. Could he have known through some inter-service connection that I'd taken my Army draft physical and should I not be accepted by the Navy I'd be on a fast track for a tour in Korea?

"So how are your eyes, boy, and the rest of you?" he asked, reclining far back in his swivel rocker, probably not eager to be required to salute me some day, and maybe even more eager to distance himself from my boots.

"Fine sir, I just had had a physical," I answered, being careful not to mention from whom.

"Look, we got lots of young fellas with great quals gunnin' for a shot at naval aviation. What makes you think you'll qualify?" the recruiter shot back.

"Well, sir, I fly a lot with my dad and sail with my grandfather on the Hudson River. I don't get airsick or seasick, so I'm sure I'd be a good carrier pilot," I responded.

"So, what's with those engineering grades?" Petty Officer Brighton asked, eyeing my suspiciously. "They don't look so hot to me."

"My dad insisted I go to engineering school, sir, but I want to fly Navy airplanes and go to sea," I pleaded.

The question and answer session continued for a few more minutes, ending with the recruiter agreeing to forward my request to his officer-in-charge, provided I show up the next morning for a physical exam and an aviation adaptability test. Relieved, I resolved to be more nattily attired, and wearing different footgear the next time we met.

And meet again we did, three days after my exam and test and in a different atmosphere.

"Um, Mr. VandeWater," Brighton began, rising out of his rocker and shaking my hand as I entered his office. "My officer-in-charge reviewed your performance on the physical exam and the aviation test and thinks you might be just who we're lookin' for. Tell ya what," he continued,

"Just sign right here and you'll have orders to flight school in Pensacola for January 1954 in Naval Aviation Cadet Class 4-54."

Wow! What a change from our first meeting, with the "Mr." thing and all. I was elated, wondering just what had made the difference. Only many years later, while reviewing all my records, did I learn that I had "aced" the aviation test and that my physical exam noted that my vision was 20/10, twice as acute as normal. It seemed that if naval aviation could use an aviation adaptable, hawk-eyed farm boy, I was their man.

And who knows? If Petty Officer Brighton ever ended up at Kingsville, Texas, where I would receive my wings, he might give me my first salute, whereupon after giving him the obligatory one dollar, I'd make it point to shake his hand and thank him.

NAS Pensacola
14 January 1954
0730 Hours

Exactly as stated on my orders to flight training, I arrived at NAS Pensacola's main gate after a drive of 23 hours from my home in Walden, N.Y., stopping only for coffee, hamburgers, and gas for my Mercury. The Marine gate sentry examined my orders, looked admiringly at my car, which was emitting a low rumble from the straight-through dual exhaust pipes, and directed me to a barracks area where NavCad Class 4-54 was gathering in the chilly morning air.

It was immediately obvious that I'd be the only student in a class of fifty-five driving a car of any kind, let alone a souped-up hot rod. My contemporaries were either clambering off buses or waving goodbye to relatives who were departing in their vehicles for the main gate. I was pleased to note that all my classmates looked sharp and physically fit, a marked contrast to the group at my Army physical the previous July. Despite my status as a vehicle owner, they seemed friendly toward me.

In conversations with my new friends, it seemed odd that about 30% of the class had never flown in an aircraft of any type, which gave me a learning advantage since I understood engines of all types, airplanes in general, weather maps, and flight planning. Yet, in two months, my classmates were performing at high levels, proving the validity of the aeronautical adaptability test.

We were assigned to a single barracks with NavCad Joe Poitevant, a former ROTC student, as our commander. A tall, rangy, red-haired Texan, Joe let it be known he had set his sights on the Outstanding Student Award which would be presented at the end of our 16 weeks of preflight training. I was designated a company commander which meant I got to lead my company on the parade ground and during our daily marches to and from our barracks to classes.

Our daily routine began with pre-dawn calisthenics, a march to and from breakfast, and a rush to ready our four-man rooms for inspection. After a full day of classes and military marching drills, we had until lights out at 10 p.m. to study and attend to our uniforms. I often joke that the only thing I learned in preflight was how to make a hospital corner with sheets on my bunk, but our classes were genuinely crammed with military and aviation subjects.

Our navigation classes taught the use of the large, square plotting boards that World War II Navy fighter planes had stuffed beneath their instrument panels. Given a carrier's position and intended movement (PIM) for the next few hours, along with wind direction and speed, we could plot our track on the plastic surface of the board and return to the ship quite handily. We learned to judge wind speed and direction by looking at the waves and wind streaks on the water and how to use a drift meter, which on many 1940s aircraft was located atop a Plexiglas window in the cockpit floor. Learning Morse code at a rate of at least eight words per minute was a must since carriers at sea transmitted Morse code characters in a magnetic north oriented circular grid. Knowing the "code for the day," a pilot could determine which sector he was in and the heading needed to return to his ship.

Our drill instructor was whip-thin Staff Sergeant Manuel Flores, one very squared-away Marine, who taught us the Manual of Arms and the finer points of formation marching.

He also supervised those of us who were marching off demerits on the "grinder," the large expanse of asphalt near our barracks that, as spring approached, became an unpleasant place, with or without a rifle.

When we marched in battalion formation, Flores was right there with us, his Korean War awards and marksmanship badges aglow, his D.I. hat at the perfect angle, his shoes glittering like mirrors. When we had our five-mile runs, he easily beat anyone brash enough to challenge him.

Flores brooked no breach of the rules. One day in ranks, Frank "Whizzer" White, pointed his rifle at an aircraft flying overhead.

"Mr. White," Flores barked, "you will not point your piece at anything you don't intend to shoot, or you will wear out your best pair of shoes on the grinder. Is that clear?"

Indeed, it was, not only to Whizzer but to the rest of us.

While I accumulated more than a few demerits during our four months of preflight, I must plead that all were the result of being "room captain," a responsibility awarded on a rotating weekly basis to one of the four room occupants. The room captain made it his business to inspect the room prior to departing the barracks. Should a roommate slip back into the room and leave traces of water in the sink, for example, that was good for five demerits…for the room captain. It was an early lesson that should the ship run aground, even when the captain wasn't on the bridge, it was still the captain's fault.

As the weeks went by, cadets developed friendships that lasted well into and beyond our military careers. Among my closest friends was "Seabo" Fuller, a Virginian, still smarting somewhat from the outcome of the Civil War, but willing to befriend a Yankee like me.

One weekend night, Seabo and I agreed, probably foolishly, that if one of us were killed during training, the other would DOR (the dreaded Dropped, Own Request, made famous in the movie "An Officer and a Gentleman"). Upon receiving his wings, Seabo joined an East Coast fighter squadron, where I later learned that he was killed on a catapult launch, his F2H Banshee crashing into the sea in front of the carrier. He would not be the last friend I would lose to aviation accidents over the next 30 years.

Surprisingly, DORs popped up our very first day of preflight training immediately after we viewed a film entitled "Carrier Flight Deck Crashes," designed, it seemed, to weed out the queasy ones. At the end of the film, half a dozen students told the instructor that they were through. I still see snippets of that film on television during military history programs where the realities of carrier aviation are displayed.

On 7 May 1954, the day the French lost their Vietnam stronghold at Dien Bien Phu, I stood on the reviewing stand at NAS Pensacola as Class 4-54's Outstanding Student, an award based upon academic grades, leadership, and military potential as our graduating class passed in review. I was elated…Joe Poitevant was crushed. We were beginning to learn about the "breaks" of Naval Aviation.

Flying the SNJ

On 10 May, I drove my Mercury to NAS Whiting Field, some 20 miles northeast of Pensacola, to begin training in the SNJ, a World War II vintage aircraft known in the Air Force as the T-6. I was impressed by how large an aircraft it was, compared to my dad's Ercoupe and Navion. The cockpit was at least six feet above ground level and the 600-horsepower radial engine was intimidating. A metal pan was positioned under the engine to catch the engine oil which continually dripped, even while the aircraft was parked. If there was no oil dripping, I was informed, the engine is out of oil...which was not a good thing.

I don't know how many SNJs were based at the several fields that made up the Navy's primary training units, but in my logbook from Whiting, Saufley, and Corry fields, from May until November 1954, I flew 106 different aircraft, all of them painted canary yellow, apparently to prevent bumbling students from running into each other. The color worked, as I don't recall any collisions other than a few scraped wingtips during the initial formation flying phase.

By mid-May, students had learned the intricacies of the SNJ and had completed practice bailout drills by diving over the right side of the cockpit, parachute and all, onto a mattress positioned on the wing. Also, we got our turn in the infamous Dilbert Dunker, a salvaged SNJ cockpit which slid rapidly down a ten-foot high ramp into a pool, stopping upside down five feet under water to give students a taste of what would be a bad situation. Navy scuba-equipped divers were on hand should a student need help exiting the cockpit and finding his way to the surface. All of us made it on the first try.

On 17 May, I flew my first flight with my assigned instructor, Lt. Finley, riding herd from the back seat. Finley was a multi-engine pilot, which was certainly not what I wanted to be. As I progressed through the syllabus, and aware of my goal to be a fighter pilot, he constantly talked to me about the joys of flying a patrol plane with several fellow crew members and the wonders of enjoying steak and eggs on ten-hour missions.

"The single-engine community shouldn't get all the good pilots," he informed me. "Why not give it a try?"

"Well, sir, I want to be a fighter pilot and shoot down airplanes, not sink submarines," I always replied, to Finley's increasing irritation.

Eventually, he became so miffed at my obstinacy that our relationship began to deteriorate. I was subjected to a barrage of trick questions and an overload of problems in the air. It didn't help that I continued to come through with flying colors.

On one syllabus flight, the student was in the back seat acting in the role of instructor with the instructor playing student in the front seat. I had heard from good buddy, Wyatt Foard, that he had harangued his instructor on such a flight, with his instructor taking it all in good humor. Aha, I thought. Here's my chance to put a patrol plane pilot in his place. Unfortunately, it didn't work out that way. During our very shortened flight, Finley became irate at my constant chirping from the rear seat pointing out how sloppy he was with altitude and speed control and, in general, being as obnoxious as I could be.

"Shut up!" he finally roared over the intercom.

Which I did, of course, realizing I was in for it when we landed. And in for it I was. Slamming the door to the debriefing room with a bang, he shouted:

"VandeWater, in my three years in the training command you are the best student I've flown with, but you can't control your mouth. If you ever acted toward a senior pilot in the fleet as you have toward me today, you'd probably be court-martialed!"

I was stunned and for once sat silent. Finally, looking into his glaring eyes, I tried to explain that I thought the whole idea of the flight was for me to be a somewhat overbearing tyrant, which my friend had said worked well with his instructor. Finley continued with his lecture about proper student behavior, but after a few minutes eased up and returned to his patrol plane pitch.

"Sir," I lied, "maybe I should look into becoming a patrol plane pilot."

Finley brightened, gave me a good write-up and we departed friends, or so it seemed. From then on, I watched carefully what I said to instructors, convinced it was best to agree with them on everything, at least until I got my commission and wings.

The SNJ was fun to fly. The big radial engine always sprang to life with blue smoke billowing from the exhaust stack for the few seconds it took to burn up the ever-present oil residue. Being a tail wheel equipped aircraft with a very narrow main landing gear, it had a marked tendency to ground loop unless the pilot quickly counteracted any deviations from the straight and narrow with rudder and differential braking. My taxi technique was good enough for Lt. Finley to ask where I placed my feet on the rudder pedals.

"They're up off the floor so I can get instant access to the toe brakes," I replied.

"I haven't heard of students doing that before," he remarked and said nothing further on the subject.

I took that to mean it was a good technique and continued to taxi that way for the remainder of my flights in the SNJ.

While not a speedster at 120 knots cruise speeds, the SNJ was light on the controls and responsive. It could do all sorts of aerobatics and it recovered quickly from spins. Crosswind landings were challenging, however, as the aircraft tended to weathercock into the wind, so we students were restricted to 15 knots of crosswind during our early solo flights.

On 28 June, after 18 flights and 24 hours of flight time, Finley pronounced me ready to solo. As usual for the solo check ride, a different instructor substituted for the student's regular instructor. I was assigned to Lt. Carpenter, a friendly, outgoing man who, after being briefed by Lt. Finley and reviewing my flight record, climbed into the back seat and off we went for Pace Field, a one-mile square grass landing area frequently used for first solo flights. The wide expanse allowed more than one student to solo at the same time while their instructors stood together watching their charges perform.

As was customary, Carpenter asked me to make a few touch-and-go landings before he turned me loose. On the very first landing I bounced the aircraft 10 feet back into the air, possibly from an unseen bump in the grass, but more likely from trying too hard, along with some nervousness. I added a little power, leveled the aircraft and greased it back onto the grass, certain that I had flunked my solo check ride. Carpenter abruptly said,

"O.K., VandeWater, make the next one a final landing."

I was devastated. Surely, I would not get to solo this day, or he would not have cut short my practice landings. My landing completed, I sat looking at Carpenter in my mirror, fully expecting him to inform me that I was through for the day. Good Lord! He's unstrapping. He must want me in the back seat for the return to Whiting Field. Instead, moving forward on the wing walkway, Carpenter slapped me on the shoulder and shouted,

"Give me three more good ones. I'll be waiting right here."

In the space of five minutes, I'd gone from devastated to delighted. For the first time in my life I was alone in a cockpit. Casting a look back, just in case he had changed his mind, I slid the throttle forward, the prop blasting the hot June air back into the cockpit. My senses seemed sharpened. The engine sounded louder, the small bumps on the field felt magnified. My flight suit was wringing wet with sweat. Flying around the pattern, I kept looking in my mirror at the empty rear seat. So, this is how it feels to be master of this big beast with my fate dependent only upon me.

Around and around I flew, making three perfect landings and ending up next to where Carpenter was standing with two other instructors. Smiling, he jumped on my wing, shook my hand and shouted loud enough for everyone to hear,

"Well done, VandeWater. Let's go home!"

Still, I remained concerned that I had not done that well and that when we got back to Whiting, he'd drop the hammer on me and demand additional check rides.

"I'm sure sorry about that bounced landing, Mr. Carpenter," I blurted out in the debriefing room.

"VandeWater," he replied, "the way you handled that landing bounce convinced me that you were ready to solo. Keep up the good work, don't get overconfident and you'll do well in naval aviation.

For the second time in two months, I was elated. First, outstanding student and now able to fly on my own. That evening at our swimming pool near our barracks, I celebrated with classmates who had also soloed that day. I not only had my necktie chopped off and was thrown into the pool, uniform and all, but I had my first beer, the first alcohol I'd ever tasted. It was not to be my last.

For the next several weeks, along with progress checks by various instructors, I flew mostly alone, polishing my landing techniques, doing aerobatics, and navigating about the local area.

At the end of July, I moved a short distance to Saufley Field to begin the formation phase of training, a must for all military aviators. Our flights consisted of four aircraft, three student pilots and an instructor. For the initial flight, an instructor rode in the rear seat pointing out the exact positions for various formations. During each mission, we'd practice breakup and rendezvous maneuvers wherein the students peeled off from the formation and rejoined on the circling instructor in a safe and expeditious manner. It was always entertaining to be joined up on the instructor and watch the remaining students come screaming in to end up overshooting the formation, which always prompting harsh words from the instructor. Every student did that at least once. Well, nearly everyone.

During debriefs, the instructor would often chide students to keep tucking it in there. You're flying for the Navy, not the Air Force, he would remind us. The standard Navy joke being passed around in those days was that an Air Force formation consisted of two aircraft going the same way the same day. We also were informed of more cute truisms, including the Navy contention that during World War II, when taking over an island in the Pacific, the first thing the Navy did was to build an airstrip; the Air Force, on the other hand, first built an Officers' Club.

True or not, such talk instilled camaraderie and a desire to best our sister service. We were convinced that Navy and Marine pilots were the best in the world by dint of being able to land aboard an aircraft carrier, day or night and in the foulest of weather. Of note are medical studies during the Vietnam conflict which proved that a night carrier landing evoked higher emotional stress in pilots than did attacking targets in heavily defended North Vietnam.

After formation and tactics training, we flew gunnery practice, firing at a towed target banner using a .30 caliber machine gun mounted in the nose of the SNJ. Hits were tallied by the marks left in the nylon banner by bullets painted in various colors which were assigned to each student.

Chapter Five
My First Carrier Landings

We began Field Carrier Landing Practice (FCLP) at Baron Field, nicknamed "Bloody Baron" for past accidents there. Fortunately, there were no accidents during the brief period I trained there. FCLP was to prepare students for the ultimate Navy experience of landing on an aircraft carrier steaming at sea. At Baron we flew the pattern at 120 feet above the terrain at 60 knots indicated airspeed. Not 62, not 58…exactly 60, which was slightly above the aircraft's stall speed. Speed control was crucial for, should the student encounter a stall at such a low altitude, there was a very high likelihood that he would crash into the pine trees rimming Baron, adding his name to the list of casualties suffered there. During the turn to final approach the student descended to 30 feet above the simulated carrier deck painted on the runway, whereupon the Landing Signal Officer (LSO) with his brightly colored paddles resembling tennis racquets became readily visible.

To this day I remember the visual signals, the preferred one being for the LSO's paddles to be straight-out, parallel to the ground (or deck) indicating that an "OK" pass was in progress. Should the pilot be coming in high, the paddles would be elevated to form a "V." If low, the paddles would drop to an inverted "V" pointing downward…a no-no which, if not immediately corrected, would be followed by a "Wave-Off," a vigorous crossing of the paddles over the LSO's head. Too slow was signaled by a patty-caking of the paddles together, the more rapid the patty-caking, the more speed increase needed. Too fast was signaled by the right paddle dropped to a 45-degree angle. If the LSO kicked one leg out to the side (even LSOs needed at least one leg to stand on) it meant unbalanced flight, a slip or a skid. Both paddles overhead jerked toward the centerline of the runway (or ship) meant the pilot was not properly lined up. If the pilot was properly set up by the time he arrived at the "ramp," the LSO signaled a "cut," his left paddle dropping to his side and his right paddle slashed vigorously across his throat, meaning the pilot must go to idle power and land his aircraft. Upon touchdown (on the old-style straight deck carriers) should the tail hook miss the cross-deck arresting wires, the aircraft would crash into the barricade cables designed to protect the aircraft already on deck. Such an accident would be an indelible mark on a pilot's record, leading to an administrative review and a possible restriction from future carrier operations. The LSO would also be subject to a review of his judgement for letting the pilot land, the usual LSO'S defense being,

"He looked good when he went by me."

On 26 October 1954, after six flights and a total of 64 FCLP passes, along with five other SNJs piloted by students, I followed our instructor out over the Gulf of Mexico to enter the landing pattern of USS Monterey (CVL-26) a veteran of World War II. My steed was SNJ-7 Bureau Number 211891, especially configured with a tail hook which was lowered by a cockpit toggle handle but could only be raised after landing by a deck crewman pushing it up into place. Seeing a carrier from the air for the first time as she sliced through the water with other aircraft landing aboard is a sight reserved only for carrier pilots, or those about to become one.

During our preflight briefing, it had been stressed that should we drag out the pattern by not turning soon enough from the downwind leg to final we would be waved off. Remember the ship's movement into the wind on the surface, we were warned, so be sure to turn early enough.

And turn early I did. On my first pass, I was so early that I was still in my turn as I approached the ramp, resulting in a deserved wave-off. Settling down, on my next six passes I saw only the OK and cut signals. I was now a qualified carrier pilot. It was a great feeling, marred only by my failure after my first landing to recognize the "unlock tailwheel" signal from the deck crewman, a necessity for taxiing clear of the arresting wires. The signal was cupped hands held over the crewman's head, palms opening and closing. I experienced a complete mental blank, not remembering what the signal meant. Finally, the frustrated crewman bounded up on my wing, reached into the cockpit and unlocked the handle, whereupon I managed a weak smile and a mouthed "Thank you." Carrier operations, it seems, have a way of cutting a man, any man, down to size.

George aboard USS Monterey
October 1954

Instrument Training

The entire month of November 1954 was spent in instrument training, alternating flights under a canvas hood in the rear seat of an SNJ with flights in the Link Trainer, an aircraft replica mounted on a pedestal.

The Link came into use in the late 1930s. It looked a bit like a child's toy, with stubby yellow-painted wings and a bulbous fuselage painted bright blue. In response to cockpit control inputs, it moved to a limited amount on its pedestal. A technician simulating an air traffic controller was seated at a control panel and was outfitted with an intercom for communications with the Link's pilot. The technician could induce thunderstorm lightning flashes in the opaque canopy and even turbulence, which rocked the Link around. The Link was equipped with an array of current navigation aids and a full panel of flight instruments. After being briefed on the mission to be flown, the student climbed aboard, the canopy was closed, and off he went on a simulated instrument flight.

The flight path was recorded by stylus on a navigation chart showing exactly where the student had flown and how precise his flight path had been, a valuable debriefing tool. Link flights also introduced a student to the effects of vertigo which often happened during actual instrument conditions in a real aircraft. One could work up a sweat in the Link flying precise patterns and fighting vertigo as it lurched about on its pedestal.

After ten Link flights and seven in the rear seat of an SNJ, our Basic Training was considered complete and students were invited to apply for the type of aircraft they wished to fly in the fleet. I chose fighters and was rewarded with orders to Advanced Training in the T-28B, which would be followed by transition to jet aircraft.

NAS Corpus Christi, Texas
19 January 1955
1330 Hours

The T-28B

After two weeks of studying aircraft systems and emergency procedures, I stood in front of the first T-28B I would fly, Bureau Number 137652. It was huge, much larger than an SNJ, with a three-bladed propeller and a nine-cylinder radial engine some 40 inches in diameter. Brand new to the Advanced Training Command, the T-28B was intended to prepare a student for transition to jet aircraft. Not to be confused with the puny T-28A Air Force version with but 800 horsepower, the B model's 1425 horsepower engine provided an initial rate of climb of 4400 feet per minute, comparable to front line fighters of World War II.

We even had lip microphones mounted on our helmets (something allowed only for instructors in the Basic Training Command) and wore oxygen masks on flights above 10,000 feet. On some missions we climbed above 30,000 feet, leaving contrails in the Texas winter sky.

Before flying solo, each student went through an instrument training syllabus of twenty-five flights under a canvas hood in the rear seat with an instructor in the front seat ensuring clearance from other aircraft. The Navy was not about to let a student loose in the T-28B without being well trained in instrument flying and in possession of an instrument flight rating.

After completing instrument training, my first solo flight was on 15 March during which I made ten practice takeoffs and landings, quite an easy task in an airplane with a wide tricycle landing gear.

Next up was formation flying, including formation takeoffs with the student flying on the instructor's wing. I was assigned to a six-student flight we nicknamed the "Plumbers." Our instructor was a red-headed, former fighter pilot, Lt. "Red" Reidle. The Plumbers flew nineteen missions together, developing a camaraderie we hoped would be replicated in our fleet squadrons.

The T-28B, like the SNJ and the P-51 Mustang, were excellent products of North American aviation. Our aircraft were new and very reliable. I don't recall ever canceling a flight due to an aircraft malfunction.

At idle power the T-28B had a most unusual and endearing staccato rumble, much like a Harley-Davidson motorcycle. There was one caution in starting the engine. Should the electric priming button be released prior to the engine receiving adequate fuel as the mixture control was advanced from the idle cutoff, there could be a horrendous backfire, necessitating a visual inspection of the aircraft's intake ducting for damage, causing embarrassment to the pilot. Of course, such a thing happened only to other students…

On cross country training flights, we cruised the T-28B at 170 knots indicated airspeed which at 10,000 feet, translated to over 200 knots true airspeed, quite a step up from the SNJ but at a cost of greatly increased fuel flow. The only downside to the T-28B was that structurally it was not as strong as the SNJ. I don't remember any incidents where the wings were pulled off an SNJ but I did learn some years later of a T-28B suffering such a fate. A graduate of Texas A&M did the trick one night while buzzing an Aggie bonfire, he and his aircraft impacting the ground not far from his aiming point.

The T-28B featured a large speed brake which allowed it to match a jet's 4000 feet per minute descent profile on an instrument approach. In the mid-1950s, the Navy could not have made a better choice for an aircraft meant to ready a student for transition to jets.

George 2nd Row 1st from Left
NAS Corpus Christi Texas
February 1955

NAS Kingsville, Texas
21 March 1955
1000 Hours

The TV-2 Jet

"So, what do you think about that little beauty, Cadet VandeWater?"

"Sir, that's the most beautiful airplane I've ever seen," I replied.

Standing next to my newly assigned flight instructor, Lt. Robert Nave, with the Texas sun glinting off the polished aluminum skin of TV-2 Bureau Number 138014, I fell in love with jet aviation. Unlike the bulky, almost bulbous SNJs and T-28Bs, the Lockheed "Shooting Star" was sleek, narrow in the fuselage, with slender wings leading to a 235- gallon droppable tank on each wingtip. An intake duct on each side of the fuselage fed air to a single Allison J-35 engine which, when moving at 340 knots, was the equivalent of 5400 horsepower. With 5500 pounds of fuel and a takeoff weight of 15,000 pounds, the TV-2 (dubbed T-33 by the Air Force) was twice the weight of the T-28B and three times that of the SNJ. Maximum speed was 600 miles an hour, again twice that of the T-28B and three times that of the SNJ. Range was 1200 miles and, when light on fuel, the little silver bird could climb to 49,000 feet, a magnum leap from my previous steeds.

In another magnum leap from my previous experiences, Lt. Nave made a suggestion.

"You realize that in less than 10 weeks you'll be an officer and a qualified naval aviator, so when just the two of us are together, I'd like to call you Ted and you may call me Bob. After all, I'm not that much older than you and maybe someday we'll fly together in the fleet where informality reigns."

"Yes, sir...I mean Bob...I'd sure like that," I responded.

And, so it was for the next 47 years until Bob's death in December 2002. We kept in touch through occasional visits and frequent phone calls. Bob with vodka glass in hand always announced himself over the phone as the "Texas Turkey," which was followed by 30 minutes of talk about the good old days. Bob always complimented me during training and afterwards, almost to the point of embarrassment, when he'd gush to whomever would listen, that I was the best pilot he'd ever flown with. I resolved to do my best to live up to his opinion of me.

I loved flying the TV-2. It was smooth, quiet, and very responsive to the controls with a roll rate of 360 degrees a second. Compared to propeller aircraft, it would go higher and faster and was simpler to fly. Push the throttle forward and it went faster. Reduce power and extend the speed brake and it slowed rapidly. No fooling with prop controls, mixture, cowl flaps, superchargers, or using rudder trim to compensate for propeller torque. The air conditioning was a godsend in a hot climate. Sweat-soaked flight suits, at least while flying, were a thing of the past.

My first solo flight was on 29 April after two flights with Bob in the rear seat. Thereafter, I flew solo during formation, tactics, gunnery (firing the nose-mounted .50 caliber machine guns at a 40-foot nylon towed target) and seven instrument training flights under the hood in the back seat. I felt more and more ready to join the fleet.

In early June, with graduation assured, each student received orders. I was stunned to learn that mine were to return to Pensacola as a flight instructor. As a brand-new ensign with a total of 323 flight hours, I'd be riding in the rear seat of an SNJ, a la Lt. Finley, teaching budding naval aviators.

Upon reporting for an early morning flight after receiving my orders, I lamented to Bob that I was being sent to Purgatory.

"I don't want to teach anybody anything," I complained. "I want to learn, and I want to go to a fleet squadron, I don't care where."

"Ted, you don't realize what an honor this is," Bob replied. "Only the very best students are returned to the training command as 'plowbacks.' Besides, when you finish your three-year tour, you'll have orders to any fighter squadron you choose."

"Three years? Bob, please help me," I begged. "Is there anything you can do to get me to a fleet squadron?"

"I really don't know," Bob replied, "but I'll give it a try."

As the orders were promulgated on Friday, I had the weekend to sort things out. By Sunday, I had made up my mind that if I were sent to Pensacola, I would leave the Navy at my first opportunity. I'd had enough of Florida and riding in the rear seat watching students make the same mistakes over and over would surely try my patience. Where was the fun in that part of aviation?

On Monday, I appeared at the flight line with what must have been a dour expression.

"Hey, Ted, cheer up we're going on a gunnery hop," Bob chirped. "Besides, there's something I should tell you."

Good Lord I thought, what now. Has my car been stolen, or what? Bob continued, smiling,

"How'd you like to go to a West Coast fighter squadron that's gearing up to get in the air defense business? Their F3D Skyknights are a little ponderous, but they're scheduled to receive the brand-new F4D Skyray, a hot little interceptor that climbs like a rocket."

There seemed to be a pattern emerging in my short naval career: highs followed by lows and vice versa. My sullen face broke into a world-class smile. I literally jumped for joy, shaking Bob's hand. The West Coast! And I'd never been west of the Mississippi.

"There will be lots of night and instrument flying you can look forward to," Bob added. "And you'll be joining World War II veterans who've made major strikes on the Japanese, been shot at, and made it back to their carriers."

Several of my classmates, overhearing all this, gathered around, clapping me on the back, some wishing out loud that they, too, could be heading for Southern California.

I don't remember if I got any hits on the banner that morning but I do remember having difficulty strapping my oxygen mask over my huge smile. That night and for days afterwards, I was still marveling at my good fortune. And I owed at all to Bob Nave. Had he not gone to bat for me, I'm sure I would have been headed for a civilian career. What a difference a few days and a little political pull can make. I'd learned a valuable lesson.

Gold Wings and a New Car
NAS Kingsville, Texas
17 June 1955
1100 Hours

"Texas Turkey"
Cdr. Bob Nave, George
Monterey, California
May 1991

"A new car? An Olds Rocket 88? Are you kidding, Mom?" I stared at the pay phone, hardly believing my ears. Mom continued,

"Your father and I think you deserve recognition for your fine performance over the past 18 months in the Training Command and we have a nice letter from the Chief of Naval Air Training to prove it. So, when will you be home?"

"I flew my last flight this morning, Mom, that's why I called. On the 21st I will be commissioned as an ensign and on the 22nd I'll receive my Navy wings. I'll get to spend two weeks leave at home and then I'm off to San Diego."

But then it dawned on me. My beloved Mercury would have to go.

"I guess I'll have to sell my Mercury, Mom, which will be tough to do, but I can't afford two cars, so I'll do it."

Which I did two days later, accepting $75 cash from a young sailor who, upon examining the engine and listening to it run, jumped in and away he went, trailing a faint blue cloud of oil smoke from each tailpipe. I had disclosed that the car was beginning to use a little oil and might need some sprucing up, but the young man was undeterred. I think he was quite taken by the extensive engine chrome.

On 22 June, during an appropriate ceremony on the steps of Kingsville's main administration building, Bob Nave pinned Navy wings of gold on my new white uniform, my black shoulder boards with the single half-inch gold stripe of an ensign gleaming in the sunlight. Bob had never married and had no family, so I guess he considered me his adopted sun. With my parents 1500 miles away, I was happy for Bob to act as surrogate.

On 26 June, after a 40-hour bus trip, I retrieved my two bags from the bowels of the Greyhound bus and hugged Barbara and my parents who had met me at the Newburgh bus terminal. The next day, I picked up my new Oldsmobile and the day after that, I became engaged to Barbara, with a plan to marry in December. My career was on a high note and I hoped it would stay that way. New wings, new car, and a beautiful fiancée. I was on top of the world.

Looking over my 1955 blue and white Rocket 88 which had 14 miles on the odometer and listening to that monstrous V-8 idle, I envisioned the fun and zest of a 2500-mile trek to San Diego. I'd be king of the road with a car that could peel rubber off the rear tires for twenty feet from a standing start. My Mercury had been peppy, but the Olds had the power of a locomotive.

At the crack of dawn on 12 July, with all my worldly possessions packed into the trunk and back seat, goodbyes said, and with a wide smile on my face, I headed the Olds southwest. My route was traced out in yellow marker across several roadmaps spread on the front seat. The next time I planned on resting would be in San Diego.

Barbara and George

Newburgh, New York

July 1955

Chapter Six

San Diego. California
Point Loma
15 July 1955
Sunset

So, this is the blue Pacific, I mused, looking westward from the Cabrillo National Monument at a red-orange sun dipping its lower limb into the sea. It was gorgeous...all that I had hoped it would be. There, one mile to the south, was my new home, Naval Air Station, North Island.

After four long days, averaging over 600 miles per day, grabbing a little sleep in the back seat when I could, I'd seen places I'd only read about. Crossing the Rocky Mountains at night, deer, very large deer, bolted across the highway and I frequently had to stop to clean bugs off my windshield, very large bugs. On the last afternoon, departing Yuma, Arizona westbound, I ran into a sandstorm that reduced visibility to a few feet and coated my new Olds with sand. That, I didn't like. And it was hot, very hot. With no air conditioning, I didn't like that, either.

I had changed into my khaki uniform at a gas station restroom on the outskirts of San Diego, but I just had to see the Pacific before checking in at North Island. Looking back to the east from Point Loma, I noticed an ugly, yellow layer of smog, even more evident at sunset, another sight I'd only heard about.

Arriving at the main gate at North Island after a car-ferry voyage from downtown San Diego, I returned the Marine sentry's crisp salute and asked directions to Fleet All Weather Training Unit, Pacific. Checking in with the squadron duty officer there, I was instructed to proceed to the Bachelor Officers' Quarters and report back at 0800 the next day to complete my check in. As it was well past time for the evening meal, the BOQ steward suggested I try the "I" Bar in the next building for a snack and a cool drink after a long day.

As I entered the bar, I was surprised to find my old classmate, Harvey Taylor, who was working on a beer and puffing a cigarette, the latter being a habit I'd never acquired.

"Well, you finally got here, eh?" Harvey noted.

"Yup, Harvey, I had a few things to do, like get engaged and shake down my new V-8 Olds 88.

"Well, that's hardly fair," Harvey retorted. "All I could come up with is a two-year old Chevy with a "Blue Flame" six-cylinder engine. Now I know where all those NavCad pay checks you never cashed went. Say, what room are you in?"

"I just tossed my bags into A-101. It seems I have a rather sloppy roommate by the looks of the place and the cigarette-filled ashtrays."

"Well, guess what old buddy, I'm that sloppy roommate," Harvey snorted. "Been here just two days myself and I didn't expect a roommate right away. Tell ya what, let me buy a beer for a rich fighter pilot. I'm stuck in an antisubmarine squadron here at North Island, flying ugly, slow, unexciting S2F prop planes. They say I'll be flying in circles at night, 200 feet above the ocean, dropping sonobuoys to figure out where a submarine is. It's definitely not what I had in mind when I signed up in this man's Navy."

And, so it went for the next hour, Harvey convinced that he'd been relegated to the antisubmarine world because of his late arrival back from his 1954 Christmas leave in Columbia. It was punishment, he said, and I agreed with him, as his flight grades were excellent. Harvey should have been awarded jets.

Fleet All Weather Training Unit Pacific

In the next week, two more 4-54 classmates checked in: Wyatt Foard and Jack Williams, both of whom would be my squadron mates in FAWTUPAC Air Defense Division flying the F3D Skyknight, indeed the ponderous beast Bob Nave had said it was. But it had two jet engines, an excellent airborne intercept radar and four 20-mm cannons with which a Marine squadron operating at night from a Navy carrier had downed several North Korean MiG-15s. No other Navy aircraft could make that claim. We'd be flying a proven killer. There were now four of my classmates at North Island, three happy, one not.

After ten instrument training flights under the hood in the back seat of a TV-2 and numerous ground training classes, on 23 August 1955 I flew the F3D for the first time. It flew quite well, although not with the blazing performance promised in the F4D Skyray, soon to arrive. The F3D's APG-51 radar picked up airborne targets at over 25 miles and the aircraft was rock-solid during instrument approaches, something we did a lot of due to the low clouds that moved in over North Island on many evenings.

All through the rest of the summer and fall, we practiced day and night air intercepts, studied air defense procedures, and fine-tuned our scramble procedures. I took great pride in being the fastest "scrambler" in our squadron of 48 pilots. From the sounding of the klaxon horn to beginning my take off roll, I could consistently clock under 2 minutes 30 seconds. My best time as recorded by our unit's control tower was 2 minutes flat. With the help of my enlisted radar operator, Bill Vincent, and our plane captain, we devised safe shortcuts to ensure I was always first out of the chocks during a two-plane scramble which, despite my junior officer status, automatically made me the flight leader.

Almost all our practice missions were vectored to the west or southwest to investigate airborne targets which were unknown to the Air Defense Command. Our contacts always turned out to be "friendlies" such as off-course airliners or errant civilian pilots far out to sea who had neglected to check in by radio approaching the California coastal Air Defense Identification Zone. Such oversights could result in flight violations and fines for the pilots at fault.

Fish or Cut Bait

While we air defenders spent many hours training, there were always a few nights a week when a young man could enjoy the benefits of living in the San Diego area. One of my favorite night spots was the Mexican Village, a Coronado bistro frequented by numerous young ladies anxious to develop friendships within the aviation community. I visited there many Friday nights, always amazed at what a fine place it was to socialize.

On occasion, some of my more fun-loving friends pointed out that, at my age, it might not be wise to rush into the vast responsibilities of marriage. It had also crossed my mind that, at age

18, Barbara might end up regretting moving so far from her family and friends and that I should convey my concerns to her. Which I did, and to which she responded by noting that she was working at West Point Military Academy, that many handsome cadets had been paying attention to her, that all her girlfriends were getting married and that I had a choice: fish or cut bait. I decided to fish, reaffirming in our weekly phone calls my newly increased interest in marriage and a life together in the California sun.

Our marriage would take place the day after Christmas in 1955. All I needed to do was to find a place for us to live and attend to a few pesky details such as getting baptized, something I'd missed somewhere along the way.

The Air Defense Business

By the mid-1950s, the Soviets posed a significant bomber threat to the U.S. mainland which prompted the Continental Air Defense Command to task several U.S. Air Force fighter squadrons with the defense of both coasts and Alaska. Any unknown aircraft entering an Air Defense Identification Zone was subject to interception and designation as hostile or friendly. The interceptor aircraft were armed and, if directed, would destroy any aircraft deemed a threat. Air Force squadrons were stationed along the West Coast at intervals from the Canadian border south to the Mexican border with one glaring omission: San Diego.

Being a major naval base for ships and aircraft, the Navy balked at allowing the Air Force to station a squadron in San Diego which some considered might "taint" the up-until-then Navy and Marine Corps town.

The answer became Fleet All Weather Training Unit Pacific (FAWTUPAC) then stationed at NAS Barber's Point in Hawaii. The unit's F3D Skyknight contingent which, up until then trained night fighter pilots, would add an "Air Defense Division" and, along with the parent squadron, move to NAS North Island. The Air Defense Division would be supported by the Navy but under operational control of the Air Force's Western Air Defense Force.

While the F3D was inferior in performance to the Air Force F-86D and F-89 afterburner-equipped interceptors, the Navy promised to assign the new, high performance F4D Skyray as replacements for the F3Ds. San Diego would remain untainted.

The on-line date for the Navy to begin providing coverage for the San Diego area was 1 December 1955. Awaiting our activation date, we continually practiced intercepts under the control of our primary Air Force radar site, call sign "Anderson."

Located east of San Diego at an elevation of about 6000 feet in the Laguna Mountains, the site had a clear view of all quadrants. With the closest Air Force interceptor squadron based at George AFB in the Mojave Desert, some 120 miles northeast of San Diego, we would have a large head start for any targets in the San Diego area.

During our five-month workup period, our pilots developed close relationships with the controllers at Anderson. Often, at the completion of a practice intercept mission, we'd be invited to "fly by and check" the two big bubble canopies covering their radar antennas, a task we happily accepted. Giving the controllers a few minutes to gather around the "bubbles," we'd fly by at 400 knots, rocking our wings to acknowledge their waves. Some of us even visited the site to see how the "other half" lived and worked. These were good times for all and we looked forward to becoming official air defenders.

A Challenge to the Air Force

Soon after our activation on 1 December, it became obvious that we would become a real challenge to the Air Force interceptor squadrons in operational efficiency. While the Air Force interceptor aircraft needed a full five minutes to become airborne after scramble initiation, our aircraft were airborne in less than three. During West Coast air defense exercises with Air Force bombers acting as targets, we consistently scored more successful intercepts. Also, on occasion, Air Force interceptor squadrons had to temporarily "stand down" until their maintenance crews caught up with ready aircraft requirements. With plenty of aircraft and a good supply of parts we didn't have that problem. Those were heady times for the new kids on the block.

Marriage and Flying

With a good attitude and a cheerful spirit, I married Barbara the day after Christmas 1955, as scheduled. I was happy to give up my bachelorhood and she was happy I did, which was certainly a good start. Odd, but she didn't mind in the least to say goodbye to her friends and family and good old Newburgh, or even her admirers at West Point, some of whom were openly critical of her choice of a Navy man.

On the second day of January 1956, after twelve hours on an American Airlines DC-7, which stopped in Kansas City for fuel and passengers, we arrived in San Diego. It was well after dark, but Harvey Taylor met us in his Chevy Blue Flame Six and transported us to Coronado. After a few days in a modest hotel there, we moved into 222 J Avenue, some 500 yards from the main gate at North Island. Our landlord was Jack Whistler, a retired Navy captain, who upon meeting Barbara proclaimed us "his children."

I was rapidly learning that a young, pretty wife is a great benefit to a man's career, something that was continually reaffirmed over my 30 years in the Navy. Barbara, a few days past her 19th birthday, was the youngest wife in our squadron. Rather than being a contemporary, she was more like a daughter to the wives and they went out of their way to make her feel welcome. That was great news for me since I could devote even more of my time to flying.

Our alert schedule was helpful in providing not only plenty of flight time but also lots of time off. We spent 24 hours on alert, flying at least once (or in my case, twice), followed by 24 hours off and then a normal workday prior to our next 24 hour-alert. It's surprising how much can be accomplished during the time when most other people are at work. The stores are relatively empty and the beaches uncrowded. I've often wished that the rest of my naval career could have followed a similar schedule.

FAWTUPAC Air Defense Division

Pilots 3rd Row

L-R Stan Fischer, Bill Pearson, Al Richards,

Bob Weaver, Vince O'Rourke, Jerry Hendricks, George VandeWater

December 1955

The Skyrays Arrive

"They're approaching the break," shouted Ensign Wyatt Foard, his southern drawl undiminished by his excitement.

Springing up from my acey-deucy game, I joined a dozen other air defenders rushing out the ready room door to view three F4D Skyrays in echelon formation approaching the overhead break for North Island's runway 29.

Led by Lcdr. Vince O'Rourke, a former New York City policeman and World War II hero awarded a Navy Cross for a direct hit on a Japanese capital ship, the sun glinted off the bat-shaped aircraft as they turned downwind for landing. As they individually turned onto final approach, light black smoke emitted from their tailpipes. We could hear the whine of their engines until just before touchdown when the pilots went to idle power. Rolling out on the runway, noses held high for aerodynamic braking, we had never seen such a sight. It was mid-June 1956 and the best fighter-interceptor aircraft in the world had arrived in San Diego.

All through the spring of 1956, I had worked hard to build up my flight time to over 800 hours, hoping for priority in training in the F4Ds, which were now the exclusive property of our most senior pilots. I often stood with my peers near runway 18 watching and listening to our World War II pilots launch in full afterburner, a sight to behold. Shortly after they were airborne, we could see the little fighters making contrails at 35,000 feet off the California coast.

Hearing and seeing a Pratt and Whitney J-57 afterburner light off was sensational, especially from 50 yards away. Our chests vibrated from the thunderous sound and it was necessary to wear ear protection.

At night, the blinding flames from the tailpipe extended for twenty feet and the sound reverberated across the bay to downtown San Diego. Never having flown an afterburner-equipped aircraft, I was hooked. I wanted more than anything to fly the F4D.

While the F3D's radar was good, the F4D's was much superior. With a flip of a switch, the Skyray's APQ-50 fire control system could be programmed for either a lead collision or a lead pursuit attack, the former being used to fire unguided 2.75-inch rockets head on at a target, while the latter provided a curving approach from the rear for a gun or AIM-9 Sidewinder missile attack. In either case, the pilot needed only to center the steering dot on the on the radar scope and fire at the appropriate range.

On 27 September 1956, I flew the F4D for the first time. Strapping into the snug cockpit was a far different sensation than climbing into the cavernous cabin of the F3D. It was the first single-seat aircraft I had ever been in. Everything was new and shiny, and everything worked as it should. During taxi, the visibility was superb and the long landing gear struts made it feel like it was taxiing on air. Or maybe it was I who was riding on air.

My first take off was at military power without using afterburner. Even then, at only two-thirds maximum power, things happened much more rapidly than I was used to. Lifting off at 150 knots, it was necessary to immediately retract the landing gear so as not to exceed the 220-knot gear limit speed. Not having flaps (the wing featured leading edge slats which automatically extended and retracted, based upon airspeed), the only thing left to do was to engage the yaw damper.

My second take off was using full afterburner. Upon brake release (full thrust would drag the aircraft with the brakes on) the throttle handle was moved outboard into the afterburner detent. After a short pause of about a second, during which the "eyelids" mounted on the rear of the tailpipe opened to accommodate the huge increase in exhaust gas volume, there was a muffled explosion as the afterburner lit and down the runway I roared, like being shot out of a cannon. It's not easy to break into an enormous grin when fitted with an oxygen mask but I most certainly did. Afterburner flying was for me and so was the F4D. To this day, it remains my favorite aircraft.

Usually, we flew with two 300-gallon externally mounted fuel tanks (which could be jettisoned for combat), two seven-shot 2.75-inch rocket pods, and two AIM-9 Sidewinder missiles but, on occasion, such as during test flights after major maintenance, we'd fly with no external stores. It was easy with 16,000 pounds of thrust, at a gross weight of less than 18,000 pounds, to achieve high angle climbs. In my favorite maneuver, which was a 30-degree banked turn immediately after liftoff and with the nose nearly straight up, I could cross over my take off point at 10,000 feet altitude in little more than 20 seconds. That was excellent performance in those days and still is.

VF-91

1st Row L-R 6th C.O. Jeff McVey, 7th X.O "Red" Leavitt

2nd Row L-R 6th George VandeWater

December 1958

Fleet Squadrons

I arrived at FAWTUPAC Air Defense Division from the Advanced Training Command in July 1955 with a total of 323 hours of flight time. When I departed in September 1957, I had accumulated a total of 1242 hours, considerably more than my peers. I would fly anytime of the day or night for the pure joy of flying. Teamed with more senior pilots, I had difficulty convincing them that a practice scramble at midnight for two hours of night flying was fun. They thought I might be overdoing it. Frequently, after a 24-hour alert stint, I'd remain at the squadron to fly a test flight or any other task involving extra flying. My squadron mates began to tease me about the thinning hair on the top of my head, suggesting it was caused by wearing my flight helmet too much.

While I loved the air defense mission, by early 1957 I longed to go to sea as a carrier pilot, so I began to petition my aviation detailer for orders to a seagoing squadron.

"Too bad," he always replied. "We need your experience right where you are."

After six months of pulling every string I could and calling him so often that he began addressing me by my first name, he relented and by September 1957 I had orders to VF-143 at NAS Miramar some 10 miles northeast of North Island. I would finally get my cruise to the Pacific and, better yet, the squadron's FJ-3s would be replaced by the brand-new Chance Vought F8 Crusader, the hottest day fighter in the Navy inventory.

Flying the Crusader was invigorating. While it lacked the agility and sports car feel of the Skyray, it easily exceeded 1000 miles per hour in level flight. Billed as the last of the gunfighters, in addition to AIM-9 Sidewinder air-to-air missiles it carried four 20-millimeter cannons, which later in Vietnam turned out to be most useful for close-in dog fighting.

Regaled by tales of the Far East by my new squadron mates and looking forward to our upcoming cruise, I was shocked to learn that, in line with Navy cutbacks after the end of the Korean conflict, VF-143 would be decommissioned. Back on the phone with my friendly detailer, I managed orders to yet another F8 squadron, VF-91 based at NAS Alameda in the San Francisco Bay area. After a few months there, another problem arose. VF-91's deployment date was to be delayed until 1960. Again, my detailer came through, ordering me to VF-154, based at NAS Moffett Field and the first squadron on the West coast to fly Crusaders.

In August 1959, VF-154 departed NAS Alameda embarked in USS Hancock (CVA-19) a veteran carrier of World War II. Her commanding officer was Captain Henry "Hank" Miller, the very same Hank Miller who, as a Landing Signal Officer, had trained the Doolittle B-25 pilots for what would be their one and only carrier takeoff on their way to bomb Tokyo in April 1942.

VF-154 shared a ready room with VF-151, an F3H Demon squadron which, with their aircraft's excellent air intercept radar, did the night flying. Our F8s, with minimal air intercept radar capability, were through at sundown. Unfortunately, or fortunately, depending upon one's view of night carrier operations, we "day" fighters were left to enjoy the latest ready room movie while the night fighter lads bumbled about in their red-lens goggles preparing for the darkened flight deck. We cheered them up as best we could, assuring them that the movie would be rewound and ready to go when (and sometimes, if) they got back aboard. We'd then enjoy the film, retire to our staterooms and look forward to sunup and more good daytime flying.

Our first stop was Pearl Harbor where we moored at NAS Ford Island. Viewing the perimeter of the island from Hancock's flight deck where battleship row had been, there was still evidence remaining from the 7 December 1941 Japanese attack in the form of sunken wrecks, including USS Arizona.

The flying weather in Hawaii was excellent, as was the liberty at Waikiki Beach, although I was surprised to see how narrow the beach was in front of the big hotels. I'd seen much better beaches in California. Besides, the constant drumbeat by local performers about how "my fodder came down from da mountain," grated on me and frequent muggings of our sailors by the locals irritated me even more. Despite many visits to Hawaii over subsequent years, I've never developed a fondness for the place.

Our next stop was NAS Cubi Point in the Philippine Islands, where we continued to train with other squadrons in Air Group 15, gaining skills which would serve us well during the upcoming Vietnam War. The weather was hot and humid, much like the summers in Florida and Texas and nothing tasted better after a long day in a flight suit than an ice-cold San Miguel beer, even while wearing that same sweaty flight suit.

Near Cubi Point was the rather shabby town of Olongapo which boasted more night clubs than anyplace I'd ever been. Young sailors, and even some older ones, loved liberty there and the local ladies appreciated the free-spending Americans who found their Yankee dollars went a long way west of the International Date Line. One windfall the Olongapo girls appreciated were regular visits by Navy battle groups which allowed the girls to establish a "Roledex" file of sorts as to which boyfriend was on which ship and when they'd likely return. While fleet visit schedules were classified, somehow the word got around.

Love Blooms in Olongapo

As an aside, in May 1968 when I was once again at Cubi Point, this time in USS Enterprise (CVN-65), one of the ship's flight deck boatswains, nicknamed "Curly" for his bald pate, fell so in love with one of the more notable Olongapo ladies (tradename, Snaky) that not only did he marry her, but held forth with a major wedding reception.

At considerable expense, Curly invited every night club girl and every sailor to an afternoon of roast pig and beer. The bride, for unknown reasons, shunned a white gown, choosing instead a tight pair of red "hot pants" with a stylish black blouse, black net stockings and black high heels. Rather tall for a Filipina and very verbal, she had a strident voice which attracted as much attention as the blonde streak in her dark hair, which seemed to be all the rage those days. Snaky also sported a feature which was not all the rage, but likely the result of some form of it. Her otherwise flawless features were somewhat marred by several square inches of her left cheek which had been subjected to acid, reportedly thrown by a rival some years prior. Once seen or heard, Snaky was not easily forgotten.

Sadly, four weeks later, when we again were at Cubi Point, Snaky had flown the coop, leaving poor Curly to find another true love. Curly made the best of it, however, holding no grudge, even when he learned that her newest temporary husband was aboard another carrier that alternated port visits with Enterprise. Indeed, all is fair in love and war, and certainly in Olongapo where there was always more love than war.

Chapter Seven
The Far East

USS Hancock arrived in Hong Kong for a port visit in the late summer of 1959. I was quite taken by the vigor of the Chinese people there. There were jewelry shops everywhere and numerous tailor shops specializing in custom made suits which could be produced in two days for about 25 U.S. dollars. There were numerous refugee families from mainland China living on the streets subsisting on handouts but, poor as they were, their small children received daily schooling. Children, still in the Chinese version of diapers, stayed busy writing mysterious Chinese language symbols, supervised by their parents or older siblings.

We fun loving naval aviators frequently hired rickshaw drivers to participate in races, cheering on our man as he pulled us through the streets. Unfortunately, some rickshaw drivers had a nasty habit of taking passengers, who had been imbibing heavily, on rides down back streets which abruptly ended when the coolie threw up the rickshaw handles spilling the passengers out on their heads and in the confusion making off with not only the rickshaw, but the passengers' valuables.

Taking the tram to Victoria Peak or a ride to Repulse Bay made for a great trip. Viewing the large number of fishing-type boats anchored in the bays, I was surprised to learn that many Chinese families lived their entire lives aboard their "junks." It was a very different world from the one I knew.

In late September, Hancock entered the Japanese port of Yokosuka and moored to the carrier pier there. Japan was a further eye opener to me. Everywhere they went, the Japanese walked rapidly or trotted, especially the women. The food was wonderfully different and good beer and liquor were cheap. At 360 yen to the dollar, a round of cocktails for a party of six could be bought for the equivalent of three dollars. Everything was scrupulously clean, although out in the countryside the rice paddies and gardens had the pungent odor of "night soil." No wonder the vegetables grew so large and tasty.

With our ship in port for two weeks, each of us were able to take extended trips to Tokyo and beyond. With squadron mate Derek Wilson, I visited Hiroshima by train, little more than 14 years after our "Little Boy" atomic bomb had decimated the city. We both wore coat and tie, even in the heat and, as far as we could tell, we were the only Westerners in town.

The Japanese women seemed relegated to second class status, walking behind their male companions who did not see fit to open doors for the ladies. Often, I detected what I took to be unfriendly glances from the locals, probably for good reason.

Viewing the Atomic Dome from a distance, we noted that while some city structures had been rebuilt, there was still much to be done.

A Strong Catapult Shot

While still moored in Yokosuka, the decision was made to launch two of our F8s to join several of air group aircraft temporarily based at NAS Atsugi Air Base. As I recall, the reason for doing so was to impress a visiting delegation of senior foreign dignitaries with the flexibility of carrier aviation.

We downloaded fuel from both aircraft so that we had just enough to comfortably make it to nearby Atsugi. I was one of the pilots selected to fly. In full afterburner, down the catapult I went and up into a nearly vertical climb that was possible at that light an aircraft weight. While the visitors reportedly were impressed, so was I. It was by far the strongest catapult shot I had yet experienced.

How the aircraft could take such punishment amazed me. In fact, some couldn't. A few weeks later at sea, the keel of one of our Crusaders was ripped out by the attached wire launching bridle during a catapult shot. The aircraft dribbled off the bow but the pilot, Lt. Sandy Button, emerged soaking wet but unhurt. Two days later, after inspection of our remaining aircraft, Sandy was again flying, none the worse for wear.

Proper Preflight Inspections

During my few years as a naval aviator, I had noted that Navy squadrons were populated by some very noteworthy characters. One such was Lt. "Tooie" Bates who gained notoriety while in VF-51, an FJ-3 squadron.

Although relatively thorough aircraft preflight inspections prior to flight were standard among most pilots, Tooie was noted for walking directly to his steed and climbing aboard with no preflight inspection, other than possibly noting that the wings were attached.

One day, a fun-loving maintenance department assigned him an FJ-3 that should have had more than a cursory inspection…it had no engine installed. The aft section of the FJ-3 detached for engine removal and sometimes, to save space, the tail section was temporarily reinstalled with the engine still removed.

Apparently not noting the unusual number of squadron personnel observing him, Tooie climbed aboard and strapped in only to find that the engine refused to spring to life. Mad as a hornet, Tooie deplaned, marched to the line shack, grabbed the maintenance "yellow sheet," and wrote in large letters:

"Aircraft down. Engine won't start."

Observers smirked but said nothing as Tooie stomped off.

The next day, as luck would have it, the very same aircraft was assigned to Lt. Bates. Doubting that the aircraft had been repaired, Tooie grabbed the yellow sheet and turned crimson as he read the corrective action, also written in large letters: "Engine installed. Starts fine". The crowd roared with laughter. Tooie's reputation was established.

Flying the FJ-3 (with engine installed) was interesting. The Wright J-65 engine made a horrendous groaning sound during the start, as if it wasn't at all interested in running that day. The cockpit instrument panel featured a fuel gauge the size of a grandfather clock, highlighting the fact that even when full there wasn't much fuel aboard. External tanks, when fitted, helped the fuel situation, but detracted from the aircraft's flight performance. Other than the F-100, which I later flew, the FJ-3's flight controls were the most sensitive I had ever experienced. The slightest fore and aft movement of the stick, especially at high speeds, gave an instantaneous responsive in pitch. At high speeds and in turbulence it was easy to overcontrol the nose position, often resulting in one's helmet slamming into the Plexiglas canopy. The FJ-3 also had a disconcerting trait at transonic speeds just below Mach 1, wherein if left or right stick was applied, due to wing warp caused by the aileron biting into the slipstream, the aircraft would roll the opposite direction.

Nevertheless, while certainly no Skyray in performance, and being the Navy version of the Air Force's famed F-86, it was tough to beat in a dogfight. I proved that one day in 1958, when at low altitude in my FJ-3, I held four F8 Crusaders to a draw, surprising the F8 pilots. I must admit, however, that three of the four pilots were new to the fleet. Had they been more experienced, I would not have fared as well.

A U.S. Air Force Exchange Tour

In December 1959, while still embarked in USS Hancock, I received orders to shore duty, courtesy of my former VF-91 commanding officer, Captain Jeff McVey, who was then stationed at the Pentagon. Jeff thought I'd enjoy flying with the Air Force and nominated me for a tour at Cannon Air Force Base, Clovis, New Mexico, flying F-100 aircraft.

The F-100 was a rather large, heavy aircraft designed as a fighter but capable of carrying a nuclear weapon. It was powered by the Pratt and Whitney J-57 engine that was in the F8 Crusader I was then flying and the F4D I had previously flown. It was an engine that I greatly respected. The installation in the F-100, however, was somewhat different in that the afterburner "eyelids" at the end of the exhaust pipe slid, rather than popped open, when the afterburner was lighted. While satisfactory below 10,000 feet, at higher altitudes the reduced 17th stage bleed air pressure often resulted in the afterburner lighting before the eyelids had fully opened, resulting in an engine compressor stall along with a loud bang which lifted the pilot's feet off the rudder pedals. The visual effect, especially at night, in the form of a large flame which shot forward from the air intake, was spectacular.

During day and night air refueling missions, we tanked from KB-50s, a version of the B-29 which was so effective during World War II. The problem was that the KB-50 was hard pressed to indicate more than 180 knots airspeed at our refueling altitude of 20,000 feet, while our F-100s could barely fly at that slow an airspeed.

As we took on fuel, we'd reach the point where afterburner power was required to stay plugged into the KB's refueling drogue. Given our afterburner light off problems, we'd often get a compressor stall along with flames from the intake which reached out towards the refueling hose, causing some apprehension among the tanker crew…and the refueling pilot.

One night, I had a rather unusual experience while refueling from the starboard wingtip refueling drogue (the KB-50 had a drogue on each wingtip and one in the tail). While I was plugged in, the tanker pilot notified our flight that we were approaching the limit of our assigned air space, so he'd be making a left turn. All went well until suddenly, the tanker abruptly rolled wings level, causing its wingtip to drop down in front of my aircraft. The resulting wing wash turbulence caused my aircraft to stall and snap roll to the left, up and over the tanker's fuselage, with me ending up to the left and below the KB-50. As my probe had disconnected properly, and I could see no damage to it, I asked the tanker pilot if I could plug in again.

"Sorry for the autopilot malfunction," he said. "Just give me a minute to get my waist gunner back in his observation bubble, as you went by rather close to him."

Eventually, the crewman resumed his station and I completed my refueling. Later, I began to appreciate how lucky we'd all been. A few feet one way or the other would have resulted in a mid-air collision, likely fatal to at least some of the tanker crew, as they had no ejection seats.

The tanker situation was eventually resolved with the introduction of the KC-135, a jet tanker, which refueled at 300 knots indicated airspeed, ideal for any receiver aircraft. The KC also would navigate during long distance flights for its flock of chicks, who needed only to fly loose formation on the tanker, enjoy the scenery and occasionally top off their fuel tanks.

My family and I enjoyed our Air Force tour in many ways but there was one thing I didn't enjoy…the suffocating regulations that governed every aspect of flying, from preflight briefing, to the mission itself, and to postflight debrief. Air Force Manual 55-5 outlined everything a pilot could and should do. If it wasn't in the Manual, you couldn't do it. Coming from what might be termed a swashbuckling Navy squadron, flying the best fighter in the world at that time and doing as I pleased, especially while at sea, I felt constrained. It seemed to me that my Air Force friends didn't know what fun flying was about.

As an example of what I felt was overregulation, I received a personal phone call one afternoon from the Wing Commander, an Air Force colonel, who asked why my canopy was raised more than the prescribed four inches above the canopy windshield bow during my taxi to the runway for takeoff.

"It was hot, sir," I replied.

"I don't care what the temperature is," he retorted. "Abide by regulations!"

During the rare unflyable days, we pilots would sit around the ready room and, rather than discuss such things as overseas places we'd visited and the things we'd learned, the senior pilot would hold impromptu quizzes, asking such questions as how many gallons of fuel are trapped in the in-flight refueling probe? One might wonder, who cares?

The landing technique in the F-100D dictated by 55-5 puzzled me. At landing fuel weights, the final approach speed was 165 knots indicated airspeed. At about 1000 feet from the desired runway touchdown point, the throttle was retarded to idle and the rate of descent managed so that the touchdown speed was at about 140 knots.

"Why not fly the approach at 150-155 knots," I inquired, "and go to idle just prior to touchdown?" "That way," I pointed out, "with higher engine rpm maintained until just before touchdown, the engine-driven hydraulic pumps for the flight controls would provide greater control movements to counter slipstream or other air turbulence."

The answer I received was that I would fly according to the Manual and any deviation was verboten. I complied…mostly.

The Tactical Air Command squadrons utilized centralized maintenance wherein all squadron aircraft were serviced by a central large facility. This has its advantages when all aircraft are of the same type, but a carrier has several types of aircraft embarked which made this system impracticable. Additionally, as each Navy squadron provided their own maintenance, they had a chance to individually excel by posting high aircraft availability percentages. I liked that opportunity.

While smothered in regulations and in an environment that, to me, seemed to stifle individual creativity, I was impressed with many of my Air Force contemporaries. They knew the mission, the aircraft, and, of course, the regulations. Captains John Searles and Herb Bryant were examples. They were excellent officers and pilots. I flew with Herb on my first flight in the F-100F, a two-seater, and was impressed with his skill in handling the super-sensitive flight controls. Other than the FJ-3, no Navy aircraft I had flown was as sensitive and it took me a few flights to become used to the Super Sabre.

The Tactical Air Command missions were interesting, especially regarding the delivery of nuclear weapons. We practiced three delivery methods, all at 500 knots airspeed: lay down, toss, and over-the-shoulder. By far the most accurate was lay down, wherein the weapon was delivered from 300 feet above the target, relying on a drogue parachute and delayed fusing to allow the pilot to escape straight ahead. The toss involved an approach to a predetermined pullup point short of the target with the weapon released at about 30 degrees above the horizon, followed by an Immelmann turn (a loop, followed by a half roll) escaping back the way the pilot had come. The over-the-shoulder delivery was similar to the toss, except that the pilot pulled up into a loop from directly over the target. During the pullup the pilot centered two needles on his instrument panel, the vertical one for directional control and the horizontal one for keeping the 4 g loop symmetrical. At approximately the vertical position of the loop, the weapon would automatically release, continuing up to an altitude of around 30,000 feet, thereby allowing the pilot time to complete his Immelmann turn and escape back along the ingress route.

The F-100 was not a great fighter plane. It had high wing loading, poor turning capabilities, and was rather slow, even in the clean condition with no external stores. Mach 1.2 at medium altitudes was about the best it would do. In my opinion, the MiGs of the 1960s, flown by even moderately skilled pilots, would have eaten it alive.

Additionally, like some other swept wing aircraft, the F-100 had a rather nasty characteristic at slow speeds should the pilot get "behind the power curve." There is a spectacular film of an F-100 with its nose at a high angle, "tail walking," just before crashing alongside the runway. Unfortunately, the pilot had gotten low and slow and, even in afterburner, there was not enough power to recover. For years, the film was required viewing for budding F-100 pilots.

Deja Vu

Near the end of my Air Force tour, my detailer offered me a choice of assignments. I could join VF-124, the NAS Miramar F8 training squadron or return to the air defense business in my old FAWTUPAC squadron at North Island, now designated as VFAW-3. He noted that VFAW-3 would receive the new F4 Phantom and remain part of the Continental Air Defense Command or disband, in which case I would be sent to VF-121, the F4 training squadron at Miramar. I felt I couldn't go wrong choosing VFAW-3. In addition, they were still flying my favorite fighter, the F4D Skyray.

By September 1961, my family and I were again in San Diego and I was again flying with a group of air defenders, all of them first rate pilots. At the time, tensions were building in the Key West area which would eventually escalate into the Cuban Missile Crisis.

VFAW-3, for some time, had provided an eight-plane, eight-pilot detachment at NAS Boca Chica in Key West. Alerts were stood in an air-conditioned trailer positioned close to runway 13 and we were assigned a hangar for our maintenance needs. We worked closely with an Air Force ground control radar site, call sign "Tarpon," manned by highly experienced Air Force controllers, all of whom were rated pilots. Our deployment tour was for eight weeks, which meant I could expect at least two tours a year in Key West.

VFAW-3 Bravo Flight

L-R 1st Row Dave Dungan, Joe Morrison, George, Dick Huston

2nd Row "Speedo" Stevenson, Ray Gurley, Lee Curry, "Mouse" Reiter

NAS Boca Chica, Key West

November 1961

In November 1961, I made my first deployment to Boca Chica, along with seven other pilots of "Bravo" flight. One pilot was Lt. Dave Dungan, who remains a close friend today. Key West was to become my favorite operating area. Not only was the flying great, but off-duty time was equally enjoyable. While not on alert, we often went deep sea fishing in a Navy boat and even more frequently quenched our thirst at bars once frequented by Ernest Hemingway.

Our alert schedule designated two pilots on 5-minute alert, two on 30-minute alert, and four on 60- minute alert. The two on 5-minute alert wore their torso harnesses and had their flight gear positioned in their aircraft. Should they be scrambled, the next crew in line would take their place as Alert 5. Our meals were delivered from the general mess and we enjoyed adequate movies and reading material for entertainment while not flying. During our 24-hour alert period, we flew at least once, either on actual or practice missions, so flight time was plentiful. Happily, we had very limited administrative responsibilities, a welcome change from squadron life in San Diego.

I relished flying at Key West. There at the southern tip of the Florida Keys, we were free of the airspace restrictions in San Diego. In the air, we could get away with almost anything. Returning from a mission, we would thunder into the overhead landing pattern at 400 knots, pull 4 g's during the turn to downwind, then hold a tight, descending spiral to touchdown, a maneuver that felt good in the cockpit and looked good from the ground.

Unlike the San Diego area, there was little air traffic at Key West and over the Gulf of Mexico, especially at night. Taking advantage of that, a squadron mate and I often practiced night intercepts on a blacked out (no lights) target, a likely situation in wartime, but for safety reasons, frowned upon by higher authority…had they known. The "target" aircraft would extinguish all external lights, while the "fighter" kept his on. Thus, the target could monitor the fighter's position and, should things get out of hand, avoid a collision by turning his lights on and maneuvering as necessary. Far out over the Gulf, with no moonlight, it was quite dark and somewhat confusing with the myriad of stars seeming to blend with the lights of fishing vessels.

The only sure way to intercept and identify a blacked-out target was for the fighter to fly a smooth approach from behind the target using his radar for guidance. Keeping the radar steering dot on top of the shrinking range circle ensured that when the radar broke lock at its minimum range of 200 yards, the fighter would be slightly below and behind the target, at which point the dim glow from its jet tailpipe (or exhaust stacks on a piston-engine aircraft) would be visible. The fighter could then close further to identify the target. To read markings on unknown aircraft at night, we carried a five-cell flashlight in the cockpit. The whole process was demanding and challenging. If the target changed heading or speed, things could get hazardous in a hurry. But that was the real world as I saw it. Of the dozens of blacked-out intercepts I ran, I was always successful. Besides, it was great fun to sneak up on my buddy and light up his cockpit with my five-cell flashlight.

Adding to the list of characters I had come to know was Lt. Leroy Stevenson whom I often flew with. Nicknamed "Speedo" for unknown reasons as he was rather short and seemed not to be too fast on his feet. Also, he was rather serious for a fighter pilot. Being a practical joker with time on my hands, I was determined to loosen him up.

One day in San Diego, at the conclusion of our 24-hour alert, I offered to call "Anderson" for a practice scramble mission. Speedo was always sure to be ready for practice scrambles, careful not to be caught eating, or worse yet, in the men's room or "head." The torso harnesses we wore were not easy to get in and out of and being disrobed in the head when the scramble horn went off was to be avoided at all costs.

Just as I was about to call Anderson asking them to initiate a scramble, Speedo dashed up and asked if I could hold off as he'd be indisposed for the next few minutes. I agreed, but as soon as he disappeared behind closed doors, I called our controller saying we'd be delighted if the horn went off immediately, which it did, and off I dashed for the flight line, laughing uproariously while looking over my shoulder for Speedo. Amused squadron observers later reported that about the time I was lighting my afterburner, Speedo burst out of the head, torso harness in disarray, his face ghost-white, believing the Soviets were inbound and we were on an actual mission, not the practice one he'd planned upon.

I was well past 20,000 feet and 20 miles downrange when Speedo checked in, quite breathless, still expecting a real mission. Informed of the facts, he was not amused, later vowing to get even with me…somehow. He never quite got over my duplicity, remaining eternally suspicious of me whenever I was close to the red scramble phone. I assured him that once was quite enough, yet all the while awaiting another opportunity, which Speedo made sure never came.

The most notable character in the squadron was Lcdr. John Hamilton, a former F3H Demon pilot approaching 18 years of service, that number alone indicating that his promotions had been a little slow in coming. "Hambone" was a Pappy Boyington (the legendary World War II Marine pilot) type of guy, short and stocky, always ready to fly and even more ready to party. John's administrative problems with his previous commanding officers were most certainly based upon his ashore performance rather than his flying abilities, which were excellent. John didn't care about rank. He planned on 20 years of service during which he'd fly as much as he could, polish his social skills, retire and never again face fetters on his behavior.

The ladies loved John's crew-cut black hair, his intense green eyes, and perpetually impish grin. To them, he was a loveable teddy bear, able to squeeze more than 24 hours of and zest into a standard day. John did everything well. He excelled at games, including dice, poker, and the Navy favorite, Acey-Deucy. I once watched in awe as he defeated all comers pitching pennies at a wall in the nifty little border town of San Luis, just south of Yuma, Arizona.

We young pilots loved his devil-may-care attitude and ready challenge of authority, although most of the squadron wives felt he exhibited "negative" leadership by keeping their husbands out until late at night. John, like Pappy, needed a war. We all thought he'd have made ace, assuming he could break away from the social scene long enough to down five enemy aircraft.

Key West was a perfect venue for a player like 40-year-old John. We youngsters were hard pressed to keep up with him. Despite his dedication to Key West fun, John never missed his alert duty. There he'd be, strapped into his torso harness, sprawled across a ready room overstuffed chair in our alert trailer, insisting he was ready to fly, although, truth be known, there were times when it was just as well the scramble horn remained silent.

John's wingman was Dave Dungan, a young Lt. as relaxed and temperate as John was hyper. John insisted that Dave accompany him on his off-duty exploits, which Dave dutifully did. Later, to our delight, Dave would relate happenings which would be unbelievable coming from any other source.

One night, for example, John challenged all patrons at a local bar to a pushup contest which ended up with John, nearly paralyzed by muscle cramps, being rushed by Dave to the Navy hospital annex at Boca Chica where the duty doctor gave him a muscle relaxant to ease his pain. It must have worked, for in less than an hour John, with Dave in tow, was back at the bar enjoying the free drinks he'd won. Who could not look up to a man like that?

The Cuban Missile Crisis

During my first and second deployments to Key West, we frequently scrambled to intercept Cuban aircraft inbound to Florida which were apparently trying to escape the Castro regime. Early one morning in September 1962, I and my squadron mate, Ron Johnson, intercepted a Cuban AN-2 "Colt," a large, ponderous Soviet-built transport aircraft which carried about 15 passengers and cruised at 100 knots. We made the intercept about 30 miles southeast of Key West at 200 feet above the water. As we were heavy with fuel and armament, slowing to fly alongside the unarmed Colt and report its markings was difficult. The AN-2 had the Cuban national flag emblazoned on the wings and fuselage and a side number which I relayed to our Tarpon controller. We were told to escort him inbound to Florida. However, after several minutes with the two of us flying close to him, the pilot abruptly reversed course back toward Havana, possibly concerned that he might be shot down.

While other Colts had made it to Florida, this one didn't, at least not on this flight. I often wonder what punishment our Colt pilot and his passengers faced upon returning to Cuba.

San Diego, California
18 October 1962
1400 Hours

Seated in our VFAW-3 ready room at NAS North Island, I listened intently to our commanding officer, Captain Robert Sweatt, describe the building Cuban crisis. The captain had just received word that our eight-pilot detachment at Key West would be increased to twelve and he needed volunteers, NOW! Having just returned in mid-September from my eight-week deployment there, I expected pointed questions from Barbara if I volunteered for this new mission. Yet even before the captain finished his sentence, I was on my feet, hand in the air, for one had to be quick in our squadron of eager beavers. Speedo, his face ghost-white, had his hand up along with several other pilots. Done deal. We'd leave the next night at sundown.

Despite my promise of dinner at the Bali Hai restaurant across the bay in San Diego when I returned, Barbara was not pleased. As she was a good Navy wife, our marriage would survive.

A Pink Constellation

Late in the evening on 19 October, we assembled our gear, said our goodbyes and, after more briefings, boarded our chartered pink (yes, pink) Constellation for the non-stop flight to Boca Chica. Our maintenance crews were also aboard.

Since the entire aircraft was ours, with nattily attired stewardesses (not yet called flight attendants) serving unlimited drinks, most of us greeted the Florida dawn through bloodshot eyes.

Upon arrival at Boca Chica, we were informed that all government quarters were occupied and that we'd be forced to put up at the Key West Howard Johnson hotel. With sixteen dollars a day per diem and a room at just eight dollars split between two roommates, we had a few dollars extra to spend at our favorite hangout, the Sun and Sand, where whiskey went for a dollar a shot. The S and S was reportedly owned by an order of nuns and was leased to a local character named George Keyes, a close friend of John Hamilton's. After many evenings of observation, many of us felt certain that, had the nuns inspected their property after sundown, they would have instantly re-negotiated the lease in favor of a rest home or an animal shelter…for the four-legged kind.

So how much better could things be, given the looming crisis? We air defenders were on duty for 24 hours, then off for 24 to relax in the sun and sand, or maybe the Sun and Sand. And the brewing conflict meant that we might see action against Soviet bombers or Castro's MiGs, which patrolled just south of the 24th parallel. For me, it surely beat intercepting errant airliners off the coast of California.

The Pentagon kept adding air defense forces at Key West. VF-41, with their new F4 Phantoms, were in a trailer near ours. The twin-engine Phantoms, later widely used in Vietnam, were new to the fleet. They featured advanced air intercept radar, air-to-air missiles (but no guns), and a two-man crew. The major problem for the F4s in the air defense business was that with two engines to start and two crewmembers to coordinate things, they were slow to become airborne. On concurrent scrambles, we'd be halfway to an intercept before the Phantoms even checked in with our controllers. Once airborne however, they were impressive, with radar able to detect targets at twice the range of ours and a speed that was double the Skyray's. Nevertheless, I was confident that on a fifty-mile intercept mission we could scramble and shoot down a hostile well before the Phantoms arrived on scene. We VFAW-3 pilots didn't lack for confidence.

Not to be outdone, the Marines and U.S. Air Force got into the game. The Marines were camped in tents at Boca Chica alongside their deadly little A4 Skyhawks which were loaded with weapons that would surely get the attention of the Cubans and Soviets. The Air Force dispatched a squadron of F-104 Starfighters to Boca Chica from George Air Force Base in the California desert which arrived in a rain squall. Unfortunately, the flight leader (and squadron commander) touched down just 20 feet short of the runway, shearing off his landing gear and closing the field which forced the rest of his flight to divert to Homestead Air Force Base near Miami.

I was flying at the time, so I missed the show, but the consensus among the Navy wags was that the old boy had done well, flying over 2000 miles and only missing his target by 20 feet. Even the Strategic Air Command bomber crews couldn't top that.

In general, aircrews in the Key West area were on edge. Air Force EC-121 radar picket planes were a case in point. One day at dawn, while making practice intercepts under the control of an EC-121, the onboard controller asked if I'd like to make an intercept using his own aircraft as target. That way, the controller would get a target's eye view of my attack, something he thought would be unique. I readily agreed since I'd never made a run on a Constellation equipped with a huge radar dome on the belly and a height finder antenna on the top of the fuselage. It was the military version of the of the Constellation we had flown to Key West in, except that it had electronic gear crammed aboard in place of plush seats and stewardesses serving cocktails and it was painted dull gray, not pink.

As I closed on the Connie from her two o'clock position, at about one mile range the aircraft suddenly went into as abrupt a turning dive a big aircraft can make. I was surprised, thinking that the aircraft commander had spilled hot coffee in his lap and inadvertently kicked off the autopilot. As it turned out, the controller had neglected to inform his commander that a friendly fighter would be making a simulated attack pass. Upon sighting me, the alarmed pilot, certain I was one of Castro's MiGs bent on his destruction, executed his escape-from-death maneuver, dislodging loose objects in the cabin and any personnel not strapped in. Discovering the truth, the commander was not happy and relayed his distress to the controller, who passed it on to me. I apologized and offered assurances that I'd be more cautious in the future. Looking back at my night refueling problem with the KB-50 tanker two years prior, I was beginning to think it best to stay well clear of large Air Force aircraft.

A Close Call

It seems appropriate at this time to conclude the Cuban Missile Crisis intercept mentioned earlier. The morning of 22 October of 1962, I was scrambled, with my wingman, Speedo Stevenson, to intercept unknown aircraft inbound to Key West from Cuba. On a vector of 180 degrees, climbing to 35,000 feet, join us as we check in with our Air Force control site, "Tarpon."

"Tarpon," Echo Lima 01 airborne on a 180 vector, gate (in afterburner), to angels 35, weapon (radar) sweet," I call into my oxygen mask microphone.

"Echo Lima 02 checking in, five-mile trail, weapon sweet," calls my wingman."

"Roger 01 flight, in trail come left to 165, continue gate to angels 37. Your bogies 165, 55 miles," comes the reply from Tarpon.

Joe Antel, an Air Force captain and the best air intercept controller at Tarpon, was a good friend. We had worked many times together in 1961 and 1962 making intercepts in calmer times, his voice always steady, comforting, easily recognizable. Joe's control of his fighters was precise, no botched vectors, his ranges to target dead on.

If you went into combat, Joe was the controller you wanted to be calling the shots from the ground.

"01 flight, your bogies have been designated hostile, I say again, hostile," Joe intones, his voice still rock steady. "Looks like two in trail, about one mile apart. They're at 38,000, 450 knots, heading 345…right at us."

"01, roger," I reply, my voice not as steady as Joe's. Leveling at 37,000, still in afterburner, just under the speed of sound, thoughts race through my mind. Is this it? Is the Cuban crisis about to rachet up to war? If so, my wingman and I will likely fire the shots heard round the world.

I peer down at my radar scope. No targets, but a strong altitude line across the scope indicating good detection capability. Although my Skyray's radar wasn't the longest-range fighter radar in the fleet, properly tuned it could easily detect a bomber-size target, head on, at 40 miles.

Suddenly, my scope springs to life…one large blip separating into two at 37 miles, right where Joe last called them.

"Joe," I slip into the informal mode we frequently used in practice intercepts, "I have two targets 12 o'clock 37 miles."

"Those are your bandits," Ted. Joe, too, has shifted to informal. "You don't need a visual ID (Identification), you are cleared to fire. I say again, you are cleared to fire."

"01 flight roger, cleared to fire, no ID," I respond, my voice betraying a building emotion, an odd tingle running up my backbone.

"02, I'll take the lead bandit, you take the one in trail. Confirm switches hot," I call to my wingman.

"02 roger, I'm still in five-mile trail, bandits just coming on my scope. Switches hot," replies Speedo, his voice higher pitched than usual.

The blips sliding rapidly down the center of my scope, at 24 miles I place my electronic range gate over the lead contact, squeeze the radar handle trigger and lock on, a large circle instantly blossoming on my scope, the quarter-inch gap in the circle indicating a closing rate of 1000 knots, the steering dot just slightly above dead center. Just a slight nose-up correction to center the dot, squeeze the stick-mounted trigger and at optimum range my weapons system will automatically fire both my seven-shot rocket pods at whatever that radar blip is.

"Joe, I have "Judy" (meaning I am taking control of the intercept). Confirm again that we're cleared to fire."

"01 flight, you are both still cleared to fire. Good luck," Joe calls, a hint of tension in his voice.

As a former F-86D interceptor pilot, Joe must be feeling the excitement and the stress, maybe wishing he was in the cockpit in my place, rather than staring at a radar scope. Fighter pilots are like that, even those temporarily relegated to a darkened control room.

Range now down to 10 miles, closing at 16 miles a minute, I lift the nose to center the dot. Odd, but I don't feel fear in the usual sense. After all, a radar blip is hardly intimidating, certainly not like an enemy with his rifle in your face, or bombs going off all around you. But I do feel immense excitement and a building tension for, if this is to be my only chance at war, I'd better get it right. If my weapons system works, if I'm good enough to keep the dot centered at the moment of firing, I'm confident that I can down any bomber in the sky. Hunched over my scope, staring at the shrinking range circle, dot centered, firing trigger mashed against the stick, in 30 seconds I'll be either a hero or a goat.

"ECHO LIMA, BREAK IT OFF, BREAK IT OFF!" Joe literally shouts over the radio, "YOUR TARGETS ARE FRIENDLY, ACKNOWLEDGE, ACKNOWLEDGE!"

Shocked, I shout back,

"01 flight breaking off, 02 acknowledge switches safe."

"02 breaking off, switches safe," replies Speedo."

Looking up from my scope, through the thin clouds I see an Air Force B-47 bomber dead ahead, slightly above me, followed by another. They flash overhead, unmolested, continuing northwest.

"01 flight, you are cleared to reverse course," Joe calls, "but be sure to give the B-47s a wide berth. They've just found out what nearly occurred and are not happy."

"Will do, Joe," I reply entering a wide left turn, my wingman joining on me as we head towards Boca Chica.

"01, after landing give me a call. I'm not sure what will become of this," Joe calls.

About 30 minutes later, I called Joe on the landline.

"Ted," Joe said, "from what I've learned, we are going to call this a 'non-event,' but do keep your notes because things could change."

"I'll do it Joe," I replied.

To this day, I have neither heard of nor seen statements regarding this incident. Although no harm was done this time, it was close to a disaster for the Air Force, Navy, and an eager young pilot.

The F4 Phantom

Standing next to my beloved Skyray, gazing at the sky, I felt my affections begin to stray. It was August 1962, a new temptress was in town and, fickle fellow that I was, I was hooked. The F4 Phantom was large as fighter aircraft go, some 58 feet in length with a gross weight of 50,000 pounds, about that of a World War II bomber. As two of them flew over NAS North Island, belching black smoke trails and emitting unearthly howls from their twin General Electric J-79 engines, I was enthralled. I'd heard of the Phantom and its fantastic performance, but these were the first I'd seen. While the visual effects of the huge plane were impressive, I'd never heard anything like the sounds of the engines. I resolved that I would fly the Phantom.

With the decommissioning of VFAW-3 in March 1963 and with the help of my ever-friendly detailer, I received orders to VF-121, the Phantom fleet training squadron at NAS Miramar. The commanding officer, Cdr. G.G. O'Rourke, learning of my interceptor background and extensive experience flying the F3D (now re-designated as TF-10B), assigned me to prepare an air training program for incoming Radar Intercept Officers (RIO's) who would be assigned to F4 squadrons. Some were Navy officers, some were Marines. With the help of squadron mate Ron Johnson, we prepared a program of 15 flights in the TF-10B which would prepare the students for the back seat of the Phantom. Our six TF-10Bs were busy day and night, which meant plenty of flying time for both of us. Cdr. O'Rourke promised that when our training program was operating smoothly, we would transition to the F4.

While I was flying the TF-10B, I managed to check out in VF-126's TF-9J Cougar, giving instrument check rides for pilot students, flying air combat flights, and making long cross-country flights on weekends…anything for additional flight time.

On 15 June 1963, I first flew the Phantom, an F4A, with Cdr. Ken Horn in the back seat as my instructor. On my next flight, four days later, I was the instructor with a student RIO in the back seat. The Phantom was that easy to fly.

Not only was the F4 huge, its cockpit was the largest I'd seen, so large that one of my shorter peers, Bill Gideon, sat on a cushion he used as a booster chair. Fortunately, the rudder pedals had enough aft travel that Bill didn't need cowboy boots to get full rudder throw.

While the Skyray was a sports car, the F4 was a steam locomotive. Starting both engines and going through preflight checks took excessive time but, once on the runway, time stood still. Engaging the afterburners was accomplished in stages, as the throttles were moved outboard in the detent and forward. As each stage "lit," there was a noticeable increase in thrust, until at full power there were 17,500 pounds of thrust from each engine. I felt strapped to a rocket. While the control stick pressures were not excessive, they were not nearly as sensitive as the FJ-3 or F-100, both of which were best flown with a two-fingered rather than a full hand grip.

While I was impressed with the speed and power, I was disappointed in the F4's turning radius. The radius was huge and, while under maximum "g" loading, the aircraft bobbled about, an easy victim for a nimble fighter such as the MiG-17. As proved in Vietnam, the Phantom had to be fought in the vertical, rather than horizontal plane, utilizing its immense power.

As a former F8 Crusader pilot, I was disappointed to learn that the Phantom had no provisions for an air-to-air 20-mm cannon, other than a large gun pod, built by the Hughes Aircraft Company, which could be mounted on the centerline station beneath the wing. Unfortunately, not only was the pod heavy but it replaced 600 gallons of external fuel. Worse yet, the gun frequently jammed after the first few rounds. I flew one training flight with the pod and was not impressed with its performance.

The F4 was easy to fly in the landing pattern, stable with extremely responsive engines. Rather than setting power by engine rpm, I preferred to use fuel flow. At landing weights, 3000-3500 pounds fuel flow per hour per engine held the aircraft nicely at pattern speeds. Later model F4s featured an automatic throttle control which could maintain precise approach speeds, a welcome feature when the pilot was under heavy cockpit workloads during night and poor weather.

In February 1964, I joined a VF-121 team headed by Lcdr. Tom Replogle who was tasked with evaluating the SPN-10, an automatic carrier landing system, in the squadron's F4Gs, which were modified F4Bs. Our mission was to fly field carrier landing approaches at Miramar, with a canvas hood obscuring the pilot's outside view, to evaluate how accurately the system could put the aircraft onto the "carrier landing box" painted on runway 24 Left.

I flew numerous approaches under the "hood," with no outside reference, keeping the system's two needles centered to a touchdown. A Landing Signal Officer (LSO) kept me under surveillance and my back seater also kept a lookout to make sure I was flying safely. It was a unique sensation to experience the jolt of a carrier-type landing while concentrating on the instruments and unable to see the runway. The system has now evolved to the point where an autopilot can fly our newest aircraft to a carrier landing touchdown with the pilot as an interested observer.

In the mid-1960s, two distinct communities emerged among Navy fighter pilots. The first and most vocal group consisted of F8 Crusader pilots...the last of the "gunfighters." They were a throwback to the old days when close-in duels were the preferred tactic. Shootdowns were accomplished from the stern sector of the target aircraft utilizing the AIM-9 Sidewinder air-to-air missile and aircraft guns. The pilots had previously flown the FJ-3 and F9F day fighters and were excellent at dogfighting. The second community, made up of former F2H Banshee and F3H Demon pilots, were night and all-weather pilots. Their preferred attack was from the forward hemisphere utilizing the AIM-7 Sparrow air-to-air missile. They populated the F4 community whose close-in maneuvering skills were rusty. While the first Navy kills in Vietnam were made from the forward hemisphere with the AIM-7, the majority of MiG kills thereafter, in both communities, were made from a stern attack utilizing the AIM-9 or 20 mm guns. In other words, the dogfight mode had re-emerged.

In May 1964, I qualified in day and night carrier landings in the Phantom aboard USS Coral Sea (CV-43). While the F4 was easier than the F8 Crusader to fly on a carrier approach, the catapult launch was another matter. At light fuel weights in the Phantom, during the catapult stroke, the stick had to be physically held back about three quarters of the way to ensure the aircraft rotated to the proper climb attitude after clearing the flight deck. Otherwise, the aircraft would settle precipitously toward the water and, on at least one occasion I know of, ended up in the water. At heavy gross weights, however, the stick had to be positioned precisely two inches aft of center. Any further back would cause a severe nose up rotation which, while a crowd pleaser to the "vulture's row" observers, was alarming to the pilot and even more so to his back seater. Since there was no cockpit instrument to tell the pilot where the stabilator (horizontal stabilizer) was positioned, it was up to the pilot to figure it out.

The problem was never completely solved, as evidenced eight years later during my VF-96 cruise in USS Enterprise (CVN-65). Our executive officer, Cdr. C.E. Myers, while overall an excellent pilot, never quite nailed down the proper stick position at heavy gross weights, particularly at night when his launches resembled a space shuttle launch with flames from his afterburner arcing up into the night sky at extreme angles. This understandably caused his back seater, Lcdr. Al Markey, consternation and I don't think Al was joking when he said that during night launches, he held his hands close to the secondary seat ejection handle located on the bottom front of the seat...just in case.

USS Bon Homme Richard (CVA-31)

In the summer of 1964, my up-until-then helpful aviation detailer called to advise me that after ten years my operational flying would come to a temporary halt, as I would be assigned as a ship's company officer aboard a carrier.

"Somebody has to operate the ship which aviators fly from," he reminded me.

While I would be able to fly four hours a month to retain my flight pay, my home for two years would be aboard ship. I was to become Assistant Air Operations Officer aboard USS Bon Homme Richard with the specialty of Carrier Air Traffic Control Officer (CATC). In other words, I'd be a sea-going air traffic control officer. I hung up, somewhat miffed, thinking that it might be time to leave the service for the airlines which, at the time, were in a hiring frenzy.

Old friend Harvey Taylor had signed with United Airlines and was assured of an early captaincy. Moping about in a childish pique, I answered a United Airlines ad and interviewed in Los Angeles. They assured me that, based upon my flight experience, I was a strong candidate and could expect to begin training immediately. Unfortunately, or fortunately as it turned out, my written Navy orders had arrived which meant that for the next two years I would not be released from the service. After grumbling for a few days, I had a shift in attitude and resigned myself to serving as ship's company. I'd make the best of it.

In September 1964, I reported to CATC School at NAS Glynco, Georgia where, for three months, I learned the ins and outs of carrier air traffic control. In between classes, I managed to fly my four hours per month in the T-34Bs based there. I took along an F4 radar intercept officer (RIO) in the back seat and, to their delight, occasionally let them fly the aircraft. Low over the pine forests of Georgia, I relished the occasional "dogfights" I had with buzzards.

Glynco's weather in the fall was hot and humid. Once finished with the CATC course, I didn't plan to return there.

Just prior to Christmas, I reported aboard "Bonnie Dick," which was home ported in San Diego, not far from our Navy living quarters. By this time, Barbara and I had three children: Jason, Kathy, and Philip, whom she'd be busy caring for during my upcoming six-month cruise.

Aboard BHR, I immediately became friends with Marine Captain Bill Ball, the commanding officer of the onboard Marine detachment, a friendship that endured until his death a half century later. Bill was a Naval Academy graduate, commissioned, like me, in June 1955. While I had been promoted to Lcdr. (0-4) in early 1964, due to slow Marine promotions Bill was still an (0-3). Such a difference in rank was a big deal in our ship's wardroom since junior officers, (0-3) and below, were served the evening meal, called "alligator chow," an hour before the senior officers dined. This meant Bill and I could not have dinner together, so I petitioned the ship's executive officer who, as senior wardroom officer, could bend the rules. Cdr. "Rudder" Keiling agreed with me and Bill thereafter attended the second wardroom seating. This, remember, was the old Navy where traditions died hard.

At that time, Bonnie Dick had three wardrooms: officer, warrant officer, and Chief Petty Officer, plus a general mess for sailors ranking below Chief Petty Officer. To the chagrin of some, in today's carriers this is no longer the case.

An aircraft carrier is a city. Within her hull and superstructure and on her flight deck there exists everything necessary to operate and maintain aircraft and provide for the crew. Bon Homme Richard was a medium-size carrier displacing 42,500 tons with a crew, counting the embarked air wing personnel, of about 3000. The latest large nuclear-powered carriers have a gross tonnage twice that of BHR and a crew of over 5000.

While at sea, underway replenishment operations are conducted several times a week. Most logistics are transferred ship to ship along cables strung tightly between them or, in some cases, by helicopters. Logistics aircraft fly aboard mail, high priority parts, and personnel.

A carrier's flight deck is among the most hazardous places to work, especially at night. Despite stringent safety precautions, crewmen are frequently injured or swept overboard. Pilots have it no easier. Over the years there have been horrendous flight deck accidents, causing major damage and often a loss of life.

Carriers operate in Strike Groups, along with several surface combatant ships, a replenishment ship, and usually a nuclear-powered submarine. An embarked rear admiral and his staff are tasked with keeping track of the overall strategic and tactical situation. A carrier's commanding officer is a captain (O-6) as is the executive officer and the airwing commander. The various onboard department heads are senior commanders (O-5), some of whom aspire to carrier command.

Nuclear-powered aircraft carriers now make up the entire carrier fleet and are remarkable ships. Later, while aboard USS Enterprise in 1968, I was amazed at the ship's ability to accelerate from a meandering ten knots to the thirty knots required to launch and recover aircraft in less than ten minutes. I was told by old hands that at full power Enterprise produced a "rooster tail" like a fast speedboat.

Aboard Bon Homme Richard, I reported to the Air Operations Officer, Cdr. Charlie Ray. Charlie was the most organized man I ever met. He kept his notes on a legal-size pad divided into sections with daily notes on each project. I immediately adopted his technique which worked well for me in the pre-computer/cell phone era. Charlie eventually commanded a large "deep draft" replenishment ship which always precedes assignment as a carrier commanding officer. Unfortunately, Charlie with (or maybe without) the help of a harbor pilot, ran his ship aground in a Caribbean port, whereupon he was removed from the carrier command list, prompting him to retire from the Navy. He was a bright and charming man whom I suspect did well in the civilian world.

During in-port periods, thanks to Cdr. O'Rourke, I was able to continue flying with VF-121 in the TF-10B and TF-9J. I also qualified in the SNB, the military equivalent of the Beechcraft D-18. The SNB had two Pratt and Whitney engines of 450 horsepower each. Although slow, the Beech was a good people and cargo hauler. With its tailwheel configuration, the SNB was a challenge to land, especially in a cross wind. To get the last few drops of fuel out of the nose tank, it was customary for the pilots to wait until the fuel pressure dropped, then quickly switch the fuel valve to another tank. On occasion, if the switch was not made quickly enough, both engines would temporarily quit, prompting startled looks from the passengers and an exchange of smirks between pilot and copilot.

In mid-April 1965, Bon Homme Richard deployed for the Western Pacific loaded with our full complement of aircraft. Halfway to Pearl Harbor, Hawaii, I had an interesting offer from the officer-in-charge of our helicopter detachment who asked if I'd like to fly in one of his three UH-2 jet-engine helos. Never having flown a helicopter, I jumped at the chance, not realizing that John thought I was a qualified helo pilot. After takeoff, John offered me the controls which I took with no questions asked. I understood how helo flight controls worked and being a former amateur bulldozer operator, I was adept at working levers and foot pedals. After a few minutes, John asked me to join up on another of his helos flying a short distance away, which I did with no trouble. Forty-five minutes later, we were called in for landing on the carrier's bow. Looking over at me, John asked if I'd like to make the landing to which I agreed, thinking he was joking for, after all, landing a helo on a windswept flight deck is not the easiest of tasks. As we approached the bow, I was doing so well that John showed his confidence by putting both hands behind his head, signaling the flight deck director that I, not he, was the pilot. Still wondering when he'd take over, but not one to quit, I continued the landing, touching down in the correct spot but with a slight bump. John kept smiling the whole time.

Back in the ready room, sharing a cup of coffee, John said:

"Pretty good flying, George, considering you're probably a little rusty."

"John," I admitted, smiling, "I've never flown a helo before today."

John's smile froze and the poor guy turned pale, bobbling his coffee cup looking for a place to set it down. He kept shaking his head, mumbling I had to be kidding. Finally, convinced that I was a fighter pilot, not a helo pilot, he cautioned me:

"George, don't say too much about this. I could be in real trouble."

I heartily agreed and apologized for putting him and his aircraft in possible jeopardy. We remained good friends for the remainder of the cruise, but I wasn't asked to fly his helos again.

In the summer of 1979, while I was stationed in Bangkok, Thailand, I told my story to the senior helicopter pilot aboard a visiting U.S. Navy destroyer, who graciously offered to let me try to land his large, anti-submarine helo aboard the ship's small flight deck. As I made my approach, turbulent air passing over the ship's superstructure overwhelmed my skill level, whereupon my cautious friend (whose hands were near the flight controls and not behind his head) took over and landed. At the debrief, Hank smiled and said,

"George, you are more than a little rusty. Stick to flying fighters."

I have not flown a helo since.

By mid-1965, the air war in Vietnam was heating up. On 17 June, two Navy VF-21 F4Bs achieved the first MiG kills of the war, engaging four MiG-17s and downing two of them in a head-on pass using AIM-7 Sparrow missiles. Unfortunately, for the remainder of the air war the Sparrows did not do as well, ending up with a 9% kill ratio, among the lowest of any airborne weapons system.

Although SA-2 surface to air (SAM) enemy missile sites were being constructed, they were not thought to be operational. Yet, on 24 July, four U.S. Air Force F4 Phantoms flying above an overcast at 30,000 feet were engaged by SA-2s, resulting in the destruction of one aircraft and damage to the rest.

Three days later, an ill-advised low-level attack against the suspected missile sites resulted in the loss of six Air Force F-105 Thunderchiefs to anti-aircraft artillery (AAA). A combination of SAMs, MiGs, and AAA were making things difficult for U.S. aircraft.

While my primary job was overseeing the CATC division, I was also called upon to prepare the daily air operations schedule, which entailed extracting mission assignments from daily "frag" orders issued by U.S. military officials in Saigon. Late each evening, while I finalized the ship's air plan, the several squadron commanding officers hovered over me, each petitioning for more than his share of missions, with me acting as referee. They were indeed an eager bunch, anxious to get on with the war and worried that we'd be headed home before they got their fair share of glory. As it turned out, they needn't have worried. They got their share of glory but also some hard knocks in the form of lost pilots and aircraft.

Bill Ball, pleased with his recent elevation to senior officer dining status, volunteered to help me dissect the frag orders. While his primary job was providing for the ship's onboard security, especially for the weapons stored on board, he had plenty of spare time. Ambitious and very bright, Bill picked up on the air warfare business quickly.

One day, during a quiet moment, he asked me to teach him chess, which I was foolish enough to do. Having been a minor chess star in college, I was chagrined that after three weeks of lessons Bill was frequently besting his teacher.

"Back to the air war," I finally told him, "We don't have time for games." We never played chess again.

Long Beach California

In December 1965, Bon Homme Richard and Air Wing 19 departed Vietnam waters for home and an extended overhaul period in the Long Beach, California shipyard. While at Long Beach, many ship's company officers were sent to various specialty schools or transferred to other fleet units, but Bill and I stayed onboard, doing very little other than watching shipyard workers perform repairs and update equipment.

The end of the day for us came promptly at 4 p.m. when we adjourned to the Officers' Club for happy hour. Our new commanding officer was Captain Gerald Colleran, a handsome man bearing a distinct resemblance to actor William Holden. The captain enjoyed happy hours immensely, although he occasionally slipped out to take a "power nap" in his official vehicle parked outside the Club.

Those summer months in 1966 were carefree and memorable. I took long cross-country flights in the SNBs based at NAS Los Alamitos, frequently with Bill as my copilot. Often, I'd stop in El Paso, Texas to visit and stay the night with my mother and my stepfather, Colonel K.C. Smith, a retired Army artilleryman who was in the initial occupying forces in Japan at the end of World War II.

While in Japan, K.C. developed an enduring friendship with Kibe, his Japanese interpreter, eventually sponsoring Kibe's daughter at UCLA in Los Angeles. A professor at the University of Texas at El Paso, K.C. was a fine host with a wealth of knowledge. Limiting himself to beer before lunch, he would shift to whiskey for the remaining hours until midnight, offering his take on world affairs, the stock market, and the government of the Lone Star State. Bill and I spent many enjoyable nights with K.C., long after my mother had retired for the evening. Up promptly at six a.m. the next day, K.C. would prepare a cheese fondue breakfast, which didn't always sit well with us during our return to California, bouncing through strong thermals along the way.

Surf's Up in Coronado

In late fall 1966, Bonnie Dick left the yard for sea trials and a return to our home port in San Diego. As was usual, prior to the next deployment, the ship hosted the families of crewmembers on a Family Day Cruise which featured air wing operations and the firing of the ship's five-inch guns at a towed target. The families loved it. Returning to San Diego we were a little behind schedule which prompted Captain Gerry to ring up 30 knots, the downside being the immense wake created which caused havoc among moored yachts and small craft in San Diego harbor and cries of "surf's up" in Coronado.

The very next day, in response to citizen complaints, we received a message directing the captain to report to Commander Naval Air Forces, Pacific and explain the reason for sailing so fast so close to shore. As the Operations Department representative, I had developed a working relation with the admiral's staff at North Island, so the Captain called me to his cabin and asked if I could "smooth things over."

"Of course, sir," I answered, ready to take it on the chin for my captain.

As it happened, things went quite well. Several staff members confidentially assured me that they were responding, as required, to citizen complaints but that they, too, on occasion, had done similar deeds. All would be well, they said, if I informed the captain that on future approaches to San Diego Bon Homme Richard slowed to ten knots well offshore, no matter how late we were. Captain Colleran was greatly relieved to escape a reprimand and promised that in my next fitness report he would note my qualities as a diplomat. Indeed, the Navy takes care of its own.

About this time, I received a call from my detailer advising that I'd finally return to the cockpit of a fighter, first reporting to VF-121 (again) to refresh in the F4 and then to VF-96 which would be making a cruise to the Western Pacific in USS Enterprise (CVN-65). I was delighted, immediately forgetting the tedium of two years of ship's company and looking forward to flying, rather than planning, missions. Barbara was not as pleased, voicing her concern that I was going in harm's way. I noted that luck had always been with me and surely would not abandon me now. Besides, should my luck run out, there was always a fine support group among squadron wives so she would be well taken care of. She remained skeptical but was "happy that I was happy."

In January 1967, I said goodbye to Bon Homme Richard and to Bill Ball who had orders to a Marine unit at Camp Pendleton, some twenty miles north of San Diego. For the next few years, we'd see each other frequently to talk about the good old days and the many hours we spent in "libraries" throughout the Western Pacific.

Back to the Phantom

It was great being back in the Phantom and I seemed to have forgotten little about the aircraft and its systems. I went through a very abbreviated ground and flight school syllabus and was returned to flight instructor status in VF-121 while awaiting the return of VF-96 to Miramar.

Cdr. Joe Paulk, whom I'd known from my previous days in VF-121, was to become commanding officer and Cdr. C.E. Myers was to be executive officer. Joe was a hulking Texan who loved to play acey-deucy, a standard game in most squadron ready rooms, which involved moving chips around a board as dictated by rolls of a pair of dice. I consistently beat Joe, which always evoked a loud roar from him and a demand that he be allowed to "get even." As third senior officer in the squadron, it was incumbent upon me to promote squadron harmony, so I spent considerable time letting Joe try to get even.

When VF-96 returned to Miramar in July 1967, they brought with them some rather battle-weary F4s soon to be replaced with newer Phantoms. In the meantime, I had a free hand to fly the old aircraft on cross-country flights anywhere I wanted to go. Given my good relations with Joe Paulk (he finally won a few games of acey-deucy), I talked him into letting me take my old buddy, Bill Ball, with me on a trip to Andrews Air Force Base in Washington, D.C.

We schooled Bill on oxygen and ejection systems and on the afternoon of 29 July, off we went, eastbound in one of the better Phantoms.

Although we had planned a single fuel stop at Tinker Air Force Base in Oklahoma, as we approached Cannon Air Force Base (my old Air Force duty station in Clovis, New Mexico), the yellow caution light on the instrument panel flashed, indicating utility hydraulic system failure. While the two primary hydraulic systems powered the flight controls, we would have no hydraulic pressure to lower the flaps, no braking action, and I would have to lower the landing gear with the emergency air bottle system.

Contacting Cannon tower, I advised them I would take the emergency arresting gear, which was a new feature at Air Force bases. Bill was as cool as a cucumber and quite amused by the situation, which was hardly dire, and we made a good approach and an uneventful arrestment. Thinking I'd have to call Miramar for a maintenance crew and parts, I was pleasantly surprised to find that Cannon, in preparation for the Air Force's new aircraft, the F4 Phantom, already had maintenance manuals and parts needed to fix our bird.

With the aircraft in good hands, Bill and I made the best of the situation by heading for the Officers' Club where we wowed the flight crews there awaiting their soon-to-arrive Phantoms with tales of the F4's performance. Upon closing of the bar at midnight, Bill and I were invited to participate in a ritual that was all the rage late at night at Cannon…pushing unattended cars in base housing from one carport to another, which the next day caused owners to wonder what had happened to their vehicles. I never understood why the Navy couldn't have come up with a cute prank like that.

The next day at noon our F4 was ready to go, thanks to the sterling effort by Cannon's maintenance crews. Asked if I wanted a test flight, I declined, saying we'd do it on the way to Tinker and off we went with no more maintenance problems for the remainder of our nine-leg trip. The Air Force might have stifling rules for their pilots but their maintenance organizations are top notch, even when working on an aircraft they had not seen before.

By August 1967, VF-96 had received our full complement of twelve F4s, all of which had been through a recent maintenance rework program that added chaff dispensers and electronic missile launch detectors designed to reduce the threat from SAMs. In September, we began working with Enterprise and the remainder of our airwing squadrons perfecting coordinated strikes on surface targets. Our sister F4 squadron was VF-92 with which we competed, sometimes on a not-too-friendly basis, often the case in air wings.

Westbound to the War Zone

In late December, we flew our Phantoms to NAS Alameda where Enterprise was home ported and hoisted aboard our aircraft from the same pier Jimmy Doolittle's B-25s were loaded aboard USS Hornet in April 1942. I hoped that my next flight would not be as final as was Doolittle's.

In early January 1968, Enterprise, with Air Wing Nine embarked, departed for the Western Pacific. Enterprise was a marvelous ship to operate from. All the systems worked…all the time. There was an unlimited supply of fresh water for showers and washing the salt spray off the aircraft, quite a relief from the "water hours" frequently imposed aboard conventionally powered carriers. The flight deck area was huge compared to the "27 Charlie" class carriers such as Hancock and Bon Homme Richard. From a pilot's perspective, the only Enterprise negative was the large, square-shaped island superstructure which housed the phased array radar system. This man-made mountain created a significant bubble of air that approaching aircraft flew through which caused a minor amount of altitude loss just prior to touchdown.

After a brief stop in Pearl Harbor for briefings, Enterprise arrived in Yokosuka, Japan on 18 January for a port visit. Prior to entering port, my wingman, Ens. Troy Nicks, and I flew two of our aircraft to NAS Atsugi in anticipation of a few days of tactics flying.

The Pueblo Affair

Suddenly, on 23 January, our tranquil port visit was interrupted by the capture of the USS Pueblo by the North Koreans. Enterprise was ordered to get underway the next day and Troy and I landed aboard as the ship steamed at high speed for North Korea.

In January, the waters off North Korea are frigid, the salt spray turning to slush on the canopies of our aircraft. We wore "exposure suits" on every flight, a claustrophobic experience for me, but a necessary precaution should a pilot end up in the water. With no alternate airfield available, every flight had but two options: land aboard ship or get wet. Fortunately, no one got wet.

Adding to tensions, every morning, three hours before daylight, our squadron briefed for what was to be a fighter escort for a pre-dawn strike on Wonson Harbor where Pueblo was being held. Yet, every day for four days, the strike was cancelled just before launch by presidential order. In retrospect, this might have been a good thing for some of us, as the North Koreans had hundreds of combat-ready MiG fighters ready to meet the fourteen fully combat ready aircraft our two F4 squadrons could provide. "Maverick," of Top Gun fame, would certainly have termed it a "target-rich environment" for our Phantoms.

A Badger Intercept

Finally, when it became apparent that no attack would be made on Wonson, Enterprise was directed to sail for Vietnam waters. During transit, as was usual, Soviet Badger bombers overflew our strike group. On 6 February, my back seater, Ens. Bill Popek, and I intercepted a Badger with the number "41" emblazoned on its nose. As was becoming common practice, we exchanged rude salutes with the Badger crew while we flew in close formation taking each other's picture. The over flight routine was a cat and mouse game. How far out could our ship's radar detect the Badgers and how close could they get before we intercepted them? While we always intercepted the Soviets a good distance out, we could have done better. We just didn't want them to know how much better. After a few minutes, I broke away with a somewhat friendly wave of mutual respect. The truth be known, however, I would have liked nothing better than to fire an AIM-9 Sidewinder into one of the Badger's large jet engines and watch the crew float down to get picked up by one of our helos and join us for dinner in the wardroom. We might have had an interesting exchange of ideas.

Vietnam Waters

By mid-February, after a one-week port visit at NAS Cubi Point, Philippines, Enterprise arrived at "Yankee Station" some 40 miles off the North Vietnam coast and immediately began air strikes against North Vietnamese targets.

At briefings, based upon evaluations by U.S. pilots of captured MiG-17 and MiG-21 aircraft, we reviewed newly developed tactics on how best to fight those aircraft. The MiG-17 was agile and had a tight turning radius but was hard for the pilot to control at speeds above 400 knots. The lesson: don't slow down and engage in a turning dogfight with a MiG-17. The MiG-21 was fast at high altitudes, very small and difficult to see but it, too, had airframe limit speeds at low altitude and serious cockpit visibility restrictions for the pilot, especially to the rear. As the Phantom had an advantage over the MiG-21 at altitudes below 15,000 feet, our crews were encouraged to work the fight down to low altitudes. From our first day of operations, every Phantom crew aboard Enterprise was anxious to engage MiGs. For some it worked out, for others it didn't.

Hot Vectors for MIG Bandits

"Showtime 603 Flight," our UHF radios crackled, "this is Red Crown. Hot vector 230 for blue bandits (MiG-21s) at 42 miles. You are cleared to fire without visual I.D." (identification).

"Roger Red Crown, Showtime flight, go afterburner and come hard port," replied our flight leader, Cdr. C.E. Myers, "Jettison centerline tanks now and check switches hot."

In unison, our flight of four Phantoms dropped our 600-gallon centerline external tanks as we passed through 650 knots, descending from 5000 feet to 3000 feet above the rice paddies near Vinh, North Vietnam. My weapons selector panel glowed green, signifying all missiles were operational and ready to fire.

It was early afternoon on 24 June 1968, and we were down to our last two days on the line before Enterprise headed home. For those of us who had yet to see MiGs, it was our last chance. "Red Crown" was the call sign of USS Jouett, a guided missile destroyer stationed off the coast of North Vietnam. I had launched as a spare aircraft, replacing one that had developed mechanical problems and was now designated as section leader. Tucked in close on C.E.'s right wing was former Blue Angel pilot, Lcdr. Frank Mezzadri. I was abeam and 500 feet to the left of C.E. My wingman was Major Jack Heffernan, our USAF exchange pilot, who flew close to my left wing, the plan being to appear as only two, rather than four, aircraft to the North Vietnamese air controllers. Now at over 750 knots, my back seater, Ens. Bill Popek, was doing his best to pick up the MiGs on radar, but only ground clutter was showing on our radar scopes.

"Showtime come right to 320, your two blue bandits are 320, 28 miles, slightly high," advised Red Crown.

"Roger, 320, 28," came 603's reply.

My excitement rising, I remember thinking that I'd finally get a shot at the enemy's best fighter.

"Showtime, your bandits are 320, 10 miles, slightly high, in a left turn," called Red Crown.

And there they were, two dark specks in a left turn, contrasting against billowing cumulus clouds behind them.

"Tally ho," I called, "Showtime 602 has two bandits, twelve o'clock slightly high. They're right in my gunsight."

"Bill," I said to Popek over the intercom, "forget the radar, I'm going to boresight lock on mode."

Pressing my PALS (Pilot Assisted Lock-on System) button, the radar antenna slewed to dead ahead and my scope blossomed into a large range circle indicating lock on, with the steering dot slightly below center, which was odd, considering that the bandits were above, but I could only hope for the best as things were happening too fast to return to search mode. At a range of 3 miles, with the MiGs now head on and slightly above, I fired two AIM-7 Sparrow missiles in quick succession. Both smoked off the launching rails, flew for a second or two and abruptly nose-dived into the rice paddies below. Unfortunately for me, but fortunately for the MiGs, still in close formation, my radar had locked on ground return below my aircraft and not on them. As the MiGs flashed by overhead, now in sight by all flight members, all four of us turned after them. Two other flight members fired a total of three additional missiles, all of which either failed to guide or detonated early.

Beginning to close on the MiGs from behind, as we approached the 19th parallel, the line we were restricted from crossing, Red Crown ordered us to break off the chase. Perfect weather, perfect intercept setup, all to naught. So now I'd go home without a MiG pelt on my belt, as this would likely be my only chance…but it wasn't.

Less than 24 hours later, on 25 June, I again launched as a spare aircraft on another attempt to trap MiGs south of the 19th parallel. This time, the flight leader was Lcdr. Jack Batzler in Showtime 613, with his wingman, Lt. Dick Earnest. As section leader once again, I flew Showtime 610, with my wingman, Lcdr. Emil Thompson, close on my wing. This time, however, things were to become more complicated, with a strong likelihood of a friendly fire incident.

Orbiting off the coast of Vinh, near the same spot where the previous day's intercept had begun, Red Crown gave us a hot vector towards a mixture of blue (MiG-21) and red (MiG-17) bandits, the new factor being that Red Crown also had two F4s from USS America under their control and on our radio frequency. Oddly, Red Crown vectored both the four Showtimes and the two "Black Lions" from USS America, toward the same intercept point.

Listening to the bearings and ranges to the bandits for both F4 flights, I became certain that the Phantoms and MiGs would end up together in one big "furball," surely a recipe for disaster. Voicing my concerns by radio to Batzler, at ten miles to go I suggested that we all get our heads out of the cockpit and scan the sky. A few seconds later, I sighted the two Black Lion F4s at our 10 o'clock in a right turn less than a half-mile in front of a MiG-21. At the same moment, Batzler called out MiG-17s below us, which were trying to join the fight. As the single MiG-21 crossed my aircraft's nose, I entered a hard, right turn, rolling out behind the MiG, about two miles in trail. Bill got a full-system radar lock on the MiG and I immediately fired an AIM-7 Sparrow, which left the rail and headed straight for the MiG's tailpipe. As the missile approached, the MiG pilot broke hard right and down, most likely alerted by a wingman, unseen by me or Red Crown. As the MiG turned, my missile altered course and continued to track until about 200 feet behind the MiG, where it detonated in a puff of black smoke. The MiG continued downward into the thick haze layer, just as Red Crown called for us to break off, as we were again at the 19th parallel.

Two days, two chances, and still no success. My frustration knew no bounds and I mumbled numerous bad words into my oxygen mask. Despite the intercept ending up a hazardous melee, once I was tailed in behind my MiG, I certainly should have shot him down. Although my AIM-7 appeared to track well, for some reason it detonated just short of the MiG's tailpipe. Assuming the MiG pilot made it back to his home base, I would guess he had as good a story as I did to tell during the evening meal.

Over the more than half-century since then, I often wonder if I should have had "radio failure," disregarded Red Crown and continued into the haze trying to visually re-acquire my target. On the plus side, I may well have gotten the MiG, as we were closing on him, Bill had maintained radar contact, and we had plenty of fuel and weapons remaining. On the minus side, we were at low altitude, exposed to flak traps, and there were likely other MiGs in the area which could have been vectored against a lone F4. At worst, we would have been shot down, while at best I'd have received a reprimand for going north of the 19th, even if I had downed my MiG. I never asked Popek his opinion, but as a young man with a full life ahead of him, I suspect he would have recommended heeding Red Crown.

Four years later, thanks to the Top Gun Fighter Weapons School and the Ault Report outlining corrections need to improve missile reliability and tactics, by the end of the Vietnam air war the Navy's kill ratio over MiGs had climbed from a dismal 1:1 to 12:1, a remarkable improvement.

On 26 June 1968, Enterprise departed Yankee Station for NAS Cubi Point. With the Marines based at Chu Lai, South Vietnam, anxious to exchange several of their old F4s for ours, I launched from Cubi Point in an F4B on 30 June, spending the night with the Marines before returning one of their very tired F4Bs to Cubi to load aboard Enterprise for return to the U.S. for overhaul.

VF-96 F4B Phantom

USS Enterprise (CVN-65)

Yankee Station off Vietnam

George 1st Row 2nd from Left

June 1968

A Drone Shootdown

In mid-September 1968, I flew the first of VF-96's brand-new F4Js which were scheduled to replace our old F4Bs. The F4J had an upgraded radar and fire control system and all the latest electronic countermeasures designed to thwart SAM missiles. It was uplifting to fly such a fine aircraft.

In late September, we began our workups for our next deployment to the Western Pacific scheduled for January 1969. During a live missile firing exercise in one of our new F4Js, I managed to down a Q2C target drone, although quite by accident. While the drone was outfitted with flares which were supposed to attract my AIM-9 Sidewinder missile, just as I fired the flares went out and my missile destroyed the expensive drone, much to the chagrin of the controlling agency.

At the end of a combat cruise, with no MiG silhouettes to paint on my canopy rail, the best I could do was to decorate my assigned Phantom with the image of one small drone.

Monterey, Miramar, and Alameda

Shortly after I was promoted to commander (O-5) in October 1968, my detailer advised me that since my current sea duty tour was ending, I would be sent to Naval Postgraduate School in Monterey, California to complete my four-year degree. The Navy required that all officers eventually obtain a bachelor's degree and it was now my turn. Disappointed that I would not be returning to Vietnam waters for another go at the MiGs, in January 1969 I reported to NPGS determined to get on with my studies.

The school's classrooms and laboratories were on the grounds of the former Del Monte hotel, a beautiful Monterey landmark. All students and faculty wore civilian coat and tie while on campus. Students had no military duties other than proficiency flying for the aviators. Our aircraft were twin-engine US-2s until 1970 when they were replaced by T-28Bs, one of which was the same one I had flown in the Training Command in 1955. The campus grounds consisted of manicured lawns and gardens and a noisy flock of peacocks, colorful but messy. As a farm boy, I did well by remembering to look before I stepped. Some of the classes were held in the main hotel building while others were in newly constructed buildings. I can't think of a more beautiful setting in which to study.

Before moving into Navy housing near the campus, Barbara and I, with our three children, rented a house right on the beach. The crashing surf rattled our chinaware and, along with the parade of watercraft, we watched furry sea otters lying on their backs in the kelp a few yards offshore. On full pay and allowances, this was not a bad way to continue one's education.

In mid-1969, the school received three 30-foot Shields-class racing sailboats intended for use by students and faculty who could find time to sail or race in the regattas held at the Monterey Yacht Club in which we held honorary memberships. Through careful class scheduling and a little finesse, I had time to spend at my favorite sport since I first began sailing on the Hudson River at age five. Spending every available hour on the water, by 1970 I was Navy sailing champion, which was nearly as important to me as my bachelor's degree. After all, the degree was little more than words on fancy parchment, while the Club trophy was shiny and had my name engraved on it.

In late 1970, my detailer called with an offer I couldn't refuse. Based on my grades, I could stay another year and complete my master's degree, after which I would be assigned to an aircraft squadron as prospective commanding officer. As the air war in Vietnam had ground to a halt as far as MiG engagements were concerned, I readily agreed.

After another year of sailing and studying, more of the former than the latter, in late 1971 I received orders to VT-21, a Training Command squadron based in NAS Kingsville, Texas, flying TA4 aircraft. Dave Dungan, my old VFAW-3 squadron mate, was to be my executive officer. While I had hoped for a West coast squadron, the training command offered first-class facilities and nearly unlimited flying hours.

No sooner had I begun making plans for Texas than my detailer was again on the phone. Would I accept trading Kingsville for San Diego, he asked? Upon hearing my immediate "you bet," he explained that the prospective executive officer of VC-7 at Miramar had been lost in a training accident and there was an immediate need for a replacement. I would report in January 1972 as executive officer and become commanding officer ten months later. While I didn't consider this an optimum way to gain a good assignment, Barbara and the children were delighted to return to the San Diego area where we had spent so many years.

VC-7 was a "composite" squadron which, in the past, had been composed of several aircraft types that provided services to the Pacific fleet, such as towing aerial targets, making simulated attacks on surface ships, providing air refueling practice, shipboard-based air intercept controller training, and various special projects such as evaluation of the ship-mounted 20 mm Vulcan gun project and a large, fiberglass towed target.

While our primary aircraft were twenty A4C single-seaters, we also had two TA-4 two-seaters equipped with the Pratt and Whitney J-52 engine, which was a step up from the Wright J-65 in the C model. Of our 19 pilots, 8 were newly arrived from the Training Command, all of them eager to fly. Our flight hours were virtually unlimited, which I took advantage of after three years of proficiency flying. The young pilots were mildly surprised to see an "old man" of 39 so enamored with flying. But fly I did. During my 20 months in VC-7, I flew 842 hours.

VC-7 A4Ds NAS Miramar

George Back Row 13th from Left

October 1973

All military units have their share of "characters," members who stand out for one reason or another. Boatswain Mate Second Class, Robert Merkle, a sailor in the old tradition, was indeed a standout. "Bos'n" Merkle, or "Boats," had been in the Navy some twelve years and was known as a wheeler and dealer. While a glance at his service record indicated an unusual number of ups in downs in promotions and demotions, he was a charmer with a ready smile and a can-do attitude. If we needed something fixed or found, he could do it.

At the time, I was interested in obtaining a Navy sextant, surplus of course, for the sailboat I planned to acquire after retirement.

"Boats," I said one morning as he stood at the door of my office, coffee cup in hand, "I don't think it's possible to find a sextant the Navy no longer needs, so I guess I'll have to settle for the cheap plastic one I've been using, which bends a bit in the hot sun."

Seeing the immediate challenge, Boats smiled and said,

"Sir, if I can't find one, it can't be done," and off he went with his sailor's ambling gait.

Two mornings later, there stood Boats at my office door with a package under one arm and an unusually large smile.

"I sure hope this will work, sir," he said. "You can't believe what I had to trade for this little beauty."

I didn't ask, but I began to understand why his promotions may have come and gone on a regular basis. That sextant sits on a shelf in my office today, awaiting more salt air. Odd, but for an unwanted instrument, it's in beautiful condition and works fine.

USS Ranger (CVA-61)

In September 1973, as my tour in VC-7 was ending, my detailer notified me that my flying days were again to be put on hold.

"Look George," he stated, "somebody has to man our ships. As a senior commander, you are up for department head aboard a carrier. Which ship do you want?"

"How about one that stays broken down in port," I joked.

"We don't have any of those," he replied, sounding irritated. "However," he continued, "I do have the operations department job open on USS Ranger in Alameda."

"Sir, I'd be happy to take that," I said, suddenly grateful for a job that even if it would take me away from flying would keep me in California.

After a few schools and numerous briefings, in February 1974 I reported aboard USS Ranger. Her commanding officer was Captain A.H. "Boot" Hill whom I had known aboard Bon Homme Richard in 1965 when he commanded an A4 squadron.

Ranger was getting on in years. She had frequent mechanical problems, especially in the engineering department, such as when one or more of the eight boilers were not "boiling."

During flight operations, the steam catapults used immense quantities of steam from the boilers and, since the ship's turbines also used steam, what little was left over for distilled fresh water frequently resulted in "shower hours," a real problem for the sailors who sweated profusely on the flight deck and in the engineering spaces.

We were one of the last large-deck carriers without a regularly assigned flag officer and staff aboard which meant I got to enjoy planning daily operations and exercises.

I was also pleased to be appointed training officer for qualifying our senior officers as "conning officer" during underway replenishments, a rather delicate task akin to flying wing on a huge oiler or cargo ship. Our goal was to maintain 140-160 feet between ships while steaming at 12 knots, which often required making heading changes of as little as one-quarter degree and varying propeller speeds by as little as five rpm. With Ranger's displacement of 75,000 tons, and in the fifteen-foot seas off the California coast, night refueling operations were serious business. Should there be a serious mishap, such as a collision between vessels, the captain was in jeopardy of being relieved of his command.

My flying was again reduced to about four hours a month in either the ship's C1A cargo plane or in whatever aircraft I could scrounge up from shore stations when we were in port. I favored the twin-engine SNB Beechcraft, a vintage aircraft still available for proficiency flying. Built for the Navy in the 1940s, it was rather low-tech but a challenge to fly well, especially during landings as it was configured with a tail wheel. The younger pilots who had never flown tail wheel-equipped aircraft had their work cut out for them in the Beech. After landing, turning off the runway at too high a speed often ended with a "ground loop," during which the aircraft spun rapidly around in one or more circles, usually eliciting a call from the control tower such as "Are you okay?"

After our 1974 Western Pacific cruise which included the usual port calls in the Philippines, Japan, and Hong Kong, Ranger returned to Alameda in October for an extended in-port upkeep period and a change of command with Captain John "Nick" Nicholson relieving Boot Hill.

During our 1974 cruise, I had found Boot to be a stern taskmaster who took delight in staying one step ahead of his department heads. Usually, I began the day at 0700 sifting through message traffic, but Boot was constantly on the phone asking what I was doing about this or that, before I had time to read all the messages. I solved the problem by reading the message traffic at 0430 every morning which equipped me with a ready answer when he called. Finally, without the fun of tripping me up, Boot quit calling. After that we got along fine, with me keeping well ahead on the message traffic.

Captain Nick was the opposite of Boot, with full faith in his department heads and a jolly attitude which transferred to the entire crew. Being aboard Ranger was now fun and Nick relied upon me as a senior old hand.

The first night at sea on our December 1975 workup schedule, I was in the wardroom when all the ship's lights went out. There had been what might be termed a "mismanagement event" in the Engineering Department, leaving only battery-powered battle lanterns to provide light in the interior spaces. Ten seconds later came the announcement over the loudspeaker system: "Ops Officer to the bridge!" I bounded up the ladders to the bridge's O-6 level to find Nick and the watch crew anxious for advice.

"George," Nick said, "we've lost power. What's your recommendation?"

"Well sir," I replied, "why not call down to the Engineering Department and ask the Engineer what the problem is?"

"That sounds like a winner George," Nick said, rather sheepishly.

Sure enough, after a few exchanges with the Engineer, the lights were back on. To this day, when we talk or exchange emails, Nick jokes about the event. Boot Hill would not have done so.

In September 1975, the executive officer, Jim Webb, and I were promoted to captain. While there were now three captains on board, there was but one "captain." When I answered the phone, I was "Captain VandeWater." When Nick answered, it was "This is the Captain."

An Overseas Offer

In late December 1975, my detailer called with the news that my next duty station would be Washington D.C. That I did not want. I'd only been there a few times and, from the stories I'd heard, the military complex there was, well, complex. Officers of my rank could expect to brew coffee for admirals and hunt for a parking place. While it was the place to be if one wanted eventual command of a carrier, the competition was fierce. Most of my peers had spent more time at sea than I had, so I thought my chances for command of a carrier were slim.

"Is there another option?" I asked my detailer.

"Well," he said, "a couple of your commanding officers think you should have a tour as a diplomat of some sort, and we have a Naval Attaché job coming up."

Envisioning a plush job in Australia or in Europe, I excitedly asked where.

"Thailand," he replied.

I was crestfallen. Of all the ungodly hot places on the planet, Bangkok was near the top of the list. Besides, I'd have to attend nearly a year of language training, ending up with a limited command of a language not very useful in the rest of the world.

"Well sir, can I think about it?" I asked.

"Don't think too long," he said, "you'd be accredited to Burma and Laos, and would travel throughout southeast Asia."

I hung up discouraged.

The next day at a Seventh Fleet scheduling conference, I met a former squadron mate, Rear Admiral Hank Glindeman, who had recently visited Bangkok and had stayed at the Naval Attaché's quarters.

"Where are your next orders to?" Hank asked.

"Well sir, it looks like I'm being cashiered. They want me to go to Bangkok," I replied.

Hank immediately became animated.

"Good Lord, George, that's the best naval attaché job in the world! Take it before they give it to someone else!"

With that, he listed the pluses:

"Your quarters come with an upstairs maid, a downstairs maid, a cook, a driver, a captain's gig on the Chao Praya River, a Beech twin-engine turboprop you'll fly all over southeast Asia and you can even take your wife along on diplomatic events. There's a two-hole golf course with sand traps and putting greens in your back yard. You'll live across the street from the American Embassy and you'll work for Charlie Whitehouse, a Marine pilot in the Pacific in World War II and a great guy. Your quarterly entertainment allowance is $2400 with Johnny Walker Red at $2 a bottle at the embassy commissary."

My jaw dropped, but I finally managed a weak,

"Gee, I never knew such a job existed."

And coming from anyone other than Hank, I would have doubted some of his claims. Gathering myself, I rushed to a nearby phone and called back my good old detailer.

"Sorry, George," Bob Rasmussen said. "I just gave the job to someone else."

"But sir," I sputtered, "I'm sure I'd be an ideal choice for the job." And I rattled on about my qualifications and my suddenly intense interest in being an attaché in Thailand.

To his credit, Bob listened, finally saying:

"You make a good case. Let me get back to you."

I rushed back to Hank, saying it looked like I might have a chance. Thirty minutes later, I answered a phone call from Washington. I didn't think it was warm enough to break a sweat, but I was sweating.

"Well, George," Bob began. "You've got the job. You'll go to Defense Language School in Monterey for eight weeks, then to Defense Attaché School in Washington and arrive in Bangkok in September 1976." We're rushing things a bit," he continued, "since there is a problem with our guy there and we'd like to bring him home early."

I was elated and immediately called Barbara, who was equally as excited. I would be joining a military attaché corps in Bangkok consisting of 26 attachés from 17 countries, each with an agenda, especially the two attachés from the Soviet Union, which at the time was a country of major concern to us.

Washington D.C.
George 1st Row 4th from Left
July 1976

At the end of February 1976, I departed Ranger, leaving Cdr. Dave "Snake" Morris in charge of the Operations Department. Over the years, I have corresponded with Nick Nicholson. He is an inspirational leader and a treasured friend.

In the fall of 2015, I sadly watched on the Internet as a large tugboat towed Ranger around the tip of South America to a yard in Brownsville, Texas, where she was broken up for scrap. I wished I could have at least retrieved the brass knob from my stateroom door, but the yard was not interested in cooperating.

In March 1976, I reported to Defense Language Institute in Monterey for my eight-week course in Thai. My native Thai teachers spent six hours a day trying to train my Occidental mind to comprehend an Oriental language. Thai is tonal and difficult to master, at least for me. Yet, at the end of the course I had reached a level where I felt I could at least converse with Thai taxi drivers and "waitresses," both of whom are important sources of information in any foreign country.

Defense Attaché School in Washington reinforced my conviction that I wanted nothing to do with that city on a long-term basis. The summer of 1976 was very hot, the traffic even then was heavy and I was most happy to graduate and leave. My classmates were headed for Defense Attaché posts all over the world. Of the fourteen, the only one I ever saw again was Lcdr. Ron Bell when I visited him in Jakarta, Indonesia in 1977.

Chapter Eight
Bangkok, Thailand

In September 1976, I drove our brand-new Honda Civic, with its flaming orange paint job, sure to stand out in Bangkok traffic, to the Port of Los Angeles for shipment to Thailand. Leaving our eldest son, Jason, (18) in Encinitas, Barbara and our two younger children, Kathy (age 16) and Philip (age 12), accompanied me to Hawaii where at Pacific Fleet Headquarters I was given an update briefing on latest events in Southeast Asia.

The last week in September, we arrived in Bangkok where we were promptly escorted through Customs by embassy personnel, our first taste of diplomatic privilege. My passport and those of my family were diplomatic, meaning we were exempt from civil laws of foreign countries. We could be deported, but we couldn't be incarcerated. Even with the curfew then in effect, we could drive about Thailand in embassy cars or our own vehicle with its diplomatic license plates. Going through Customs, our baggage and personal effects were not subject to inspection, whether entering or leaving the country. While it was a privilege, it was also a responsibility to ensure that we were not breaking any laws.

My predecessor, Captain Ed Graham, was a 1946 graduate of the U.S. Naval Academy and a classmate of President Jimmy Carter. He was a take-no-prisoners type of guy, intent on his perquisites and at odds with the Defense Attaché, Air Force Colonel Bob Koernig, who was in charge of the Bangkok Defense Attaché Office. They did not see eye to eye on most issues and barely spoke to each other.

Upon my arrival, each immediately briefed me that the other was a scoundrel and not to be trusted. As I had been informed by DIA of the friction between the two prior to my arrival, I merely listened to each in turn and nodded my head, confident that things would change for the better when they both departed for home.

Koernig's replacement was Air Force Colonel Jim Diddle, senior to me by a few numbers, whom I had met at Defense Language Institute in Monterey. A former B-47 pilot, Jim was normally amiable but had some type of genetic defect (he later claimed), which affected his behavior when he drank liquor, not a preferred characteristic for an attaché who would be expected to attend many diplomatic and social events where liquor flowed freely. Jim was a golf addict and made it his goal to play every golf course in Thailand. As our Beech Kingair C-12A required two pilots, he and I frequently flew together on golfing junkets disguised as official business.

One golf course of note was at Khoa Yai, a forest reserve in the mountains of central Thailand, which also happened to be home to some 50 tigers. Occasionally, we were told, one would be seen crossing the links after sundown. Just prior to the first time we played there, a tiger had killed and eaten a young girl. Later killed by forestry officials, it proved to be a male over nine feet in length weighing 440 pounds. Considering not only the tiger threat, but also the resident cobras, one had to be careful not to send his caddy into the jungle after an errant golf ball lest the golfer end up carrying his own golf clubs.

While our quarters were being readied after the Grahams' departure, our family stayed at the lovely Erawan Hotel, a few blocks from the American Embassy. Each weekday my driver, Prayoon, transported me to and from the embassy and around town as required. He also provided transportation for Barbara during her social calls on the wives of senior Royal Thai Navy officers and the wives of members of the Military Attaché Corps. Our quarters, in a gated compound across Wireless Road from the embassy, were fully air conditioned with four bedrooms and four baths, plus large living and dining rooms needed to properly entertain the many guests we could expect.

As Hank had said, the back yard did indeed feature a two-hole golf course complete with sand traps which we frequently used while entertaining our guests. While I was never enthralled with golf, it seemed I was in the distinct minority, as every senior military and diplomatic officer in Thailand I ever met was a golf enthusiast.

We kept the same household help that the Grahams had spoken so highly of. "Jerry" was our full-time, live-in cook who also did the shopping at local food markets. She was an excellent chef able to prepare Thai or American menus on short notice. Her monthly salary was the equivalent of $45 dollars. "Deng," our full-time maid, was married and lived at home, but spent all day and often all evening in our quarters attending to our guests. She was paid $30 a month. Jerry at age 50 was a bit superstitious and old fashioned, while Deng, only 30, was of a different generation and modern in habits and attitudes. During our four-year tour, both became like family to us.

L-R Barbara, "Jerry," George, "Deng"
Loi Krathong Celebration
Bangkok, Thailand
November 1977

The Attaché Business

The American embassy in Bangkok and the two consulates, one in Chiang Mai 500 miles to the north and one in Songkhla, 500 miles south near the Malaysian border, employed nearly 300 personnel, most of whom populated the usual array of State Department offices. Our ambassador was Charles Whitehouse, an old Southeast Asia hand, who in 1978 was replaced by Morton Abramowitz. Although they were quite different, I liked them both. If they needed a lift in our C-12A aircraft, I could always fit them in and call it a military mission. Charlie was of the Virginia Hunt Club crowd, while Mort was a young gun of the next generation.

The Defense Attaché Office, housed within the embassy, consisted of six attachés. Air Force Colonel Jim Diddle, the senior member, was assisted by Air Force Major Jack Zimmerman, who in 1977 was succeeded by Air Force Lt. Col. Don Cann.

As Naval Attaché and second senior officer, my assistant was Marine Major Burt Sperry, also a naval aviator.

Colonel Mack McGahee, succeeded in 1980 by Colonel "Stump" Joseph, was the Army Attaché who was assisted by Army Lt. Col. Steve Alpern, who in turn was replaced in 1977 by Lt. Col. George McQuillen.

The Army members all were on their second tours in Thailand and spoke Thai fluently. Alpern and McQuillen were particularly skilled in the language, often partying late into the evening with their Thai Army counterparts, singing Thai songs and gleaning information not available in more formal settings. In comparison, the Air Force team, except for Zimmerman who was quite fluent, spoke limited Thai and my Navy team stuck mostly to English. Fortunately, the Thai military officers we dealt with spoke good to excellent English, as did the 26 members of the Military Attaché Corps in Thailand (MACT).

The job of U.S. military attachés in the many posts around the world is to gather military intelligence on the host country and other countries in the region by overt means while in military uniform. Unlike the CIA, which has vast funds to pay for information and to support clandestine agents, DIA's military attachés gain information from personal friendships and, other than paying for a few cocktails or hosting dinner parties, disburse no funds. Attachés are expected to attend military and diplomatic events such as "National Days," during which various embassies celebrated with large parties. On occasion, Barbara and I attended as many as five events in one evening which made us appreciate a sober embassy driver familiar with Bangkok.

Each month, the MACT held a luncheon hosted in turn by the members. The attaché who was longest in Thailand was designated Dean and was responsible for making formal arrangements to visit Thai military bases and for maintaining contacts with high ranking Thai officers, along with managing the affairs of the MACT.

In mid-1980 I was designated Dean. As there were among us attachés from nations not friendly towards each other, I was careful in my seating arrangements at our luncheons. The Israeli did not sit next to the Soviets and there were tensions between the Soviets and the Chinese. The Peoples Republic of China Defense Attaché, Mr. Mao Hsien-chai, was always dressed in a "Mao" jacket and, in my mind, appeared rather inscrutable. He was suspected by some of us to be a general officer in the People's Army. Allegedly, he spoke no English so conversations with him were funneled through his interpreter, Mr. Jo, who spoke excellent English and probably a few other languages. Some of us thought Mr. Mao understood more English than he let on. For example, when asked a probing question in English, we noted that he sometimes winced, even before Mr. Jo began the translation.

I enjoyed sparring with Soviet Defense Attaché, Colonel Anatoli Gouriev, a former MiG-21 pilot. I accused him of flying with the North Vietnamese during the Vietnam war but, as the good colonel insisted otherwise, I saw no point in pressing the issue. Gouriev's assistant was naval officer Lcdr. Yuri Ignatiev, a friendly 32-year old, easy to talk with, who expressed much greater interest in Western ways than did his boss. At intervals, we noted each of the Soviets were recalled to Moscow for briefings which some of us thought might be a check upon their loyalty.

While our primary job as attachés was collecting military intelligence, we were also representatives of our branches of the service and as such were often called upon to give advice of a military nature to the ambassador and his staff. Additionally, we were tasked to coordinate visits to our host country by high-ranking members of our respective services and, in my case, U.S. Navy ship visits.

During Defense Attaché School, it had been made abundantly clear to me that if a U.S. Navy ship visited Thailand, I would be the main coordinator. That point was forcefully driven home during a briefing by none other than the father of our nuclear Navy, Admiral Hyman Rickover, who stormed into our briefing room in an ill-fitting khaki uniform, devoid of military rank and a belt much too long for his waist. Glaring at us, he said by way of introduction,

"I don't care what you think, but to me you're nothing but a bunch of goddamn spies! When my nuclear ships call in your country, you had best put all else aside or in two weeks you'll have orders to a place you won't like!"

Those who have seen the movie "Top Gun," wherein the Air Wing Commander threatened Maverick and Goose with an assignment flying rubber items out of Hong Kong, would understand our startled reaction. After a further harangue and fielding no questions, the admiral spun on his heel and stomped out of the room, slamming the door. His flag aide, a Navy captain, delayed just long enough to whisper,

"The admiral is having a bad day."

As I found during nuclear ship and submarine visits to Thailand, Rickover's officers lived in fear of a midnight phone call from him, asking what had been done about this or that or, worse yet, being summarily relieved of command. Most of his captains would not leave their ships for more than an hour or two when on a port visit, with one noteworthy exception, Cdr. Milo Daughters, skipper of the nuclear attack submarine USS Queenfish (SSN-651).

In late 1979, Queenfish called at Sattahip, the only port the Royal Thai Navy allowed nuclear-powered ships to visit. Burt Sperry and I were on hand to welcome her. Standing on the pier, I was immediately impressed with Milo's panache as he stood on his sub's starboard sail, waving a large cigar, while directing docking maneuvers.

"Burt," I said, "this skipper acts more like a fighter pilot than a nuclear sailor worried about a call from Rickover."

Burt, also a fighter pilot, agreed. As soon as the final line was made fast to the bollards, onto the pier bounded Milo. Sporting a big smile and still holding his cigar, he asked,

"When do we start for Pattaya Beach, sir? I'm looking forward to meeting my wife there."

"Right away, Milo," I said, "We can also arrange for your return back here later today."

"Return for what?" he asked, slightly puzzled.

"Well," I replied, "all our other nuclear skippers make two hours the maximum time they will be away from their ship."

"Captain VandeWater," he said, "that's why I have an executive officer. If he can't hack it, I'll fire him and get someone who can!"

Turning to Burt I said,

"I think Cdr. Daughters missed his calling. He should have been a fighter pilot."

Burt nodded his agreement as Milo headed for my sedan which would take him to Pattaya for however long he wished to stay. As he clambered into the back seat, still smiling, Queenfish's skipper said,

"Sir, I sure do appreciate your kind words about being a fighter pilot, but then, I would never have met the father of our nuclear Navy," his smile fading somewhat.

Milo Daughters was one of a kind. His crew loved him, and his performance record indicated he was a "hot runner" destined for flag rank at an early age.

Less than a year later, while playing tennis with Barbara at Barbers Point, Hawaii, enroute to the U.S. at the end of our attaché tour, I noticed a pale-skinned gentleman in the next court who likely was a submariner not often exposed to sunlight. He acknowledging that he was so I asked if by chance he knew Milo Daughters. He rested his racquet on the clay and stood silent for a moment before replying,

"Milo had a fatal heart attack in San Diego on 6 November. I was at his party celebrating Milo's recent selection to captain, when he collapsed at our table and could not be revived."

It was my turn to remain silent.

"I'm greatly saddened," I finally managed. "I'd like to tell him again he'd have been a great fighter pilot."

Milo was 39 years old.

Thai Prime Minister Gen. Kriangsak 1st Row 4th from Left
U.S. Ambassador Abramowitz 1st Row 6th from Left. George Back Row 2nd from Left.
USS Midway (CVA-41)
Off Pattaya Beach Thailand
December 1978

Hosting the U.S. Navy

During my four-year tour, 120 U.S. Navy ships called at Pattaya, Sattahip, Phuket, and Bangkok. On several occasions, an entire carrier battle group (now called a strike group) with as many as seven ships and some 8000 crewmembers called at Pattaya.

I made it a point to visit each ship to brief the crews via their internal ship's TV system on the joys, and sometimes the woes, awaiting them ashore. I also escorted each ship's captain and the occasional flag officer on calls to senior Thai officials and introduced each to our ambassador.

One of my cautions for thirsty sailors ashore after many weeks at sea was that the local Thai beer had twice the alcohol content of American brews. A combination of hot sun and several bottles of Singha or Amarit beer often resulted in rowdy behavior and a trip to the local Thai jail, an unpleasant way to spend precious liberty hours. Burt Sperry became adept at negotiating the release of the, by then, quite sober miscreants. Of course, there were always fines to be paid, usually by the ship's Welfare and Recreation funds, later to be extracted from the sailor himself. I was also explicit about the hazards found in local bars and massage parlors where young ladies plied the oldest of professions.

One source of fun for crew members involved "water scooters," water-jet-powered small watercraft with top speeds of over 30 mph. The most fun appeared to be water-borne dogfights and games of chicken, often resulting in bruised sailors and sunken scooters. The scooter owners would then appear at the ships' quarterdecks demanding payment, usually provided by the good old Welfare and Recreation kitty.

Once the ships left port, the enterprising scooter owners winched up their craft from the 60-foot-deep water and slapped fiberglass patches on the scooters in time for the arrival of more water sports enthusiasts.

All in all, the crews behaved well and enjoyed their visits, as did the Thai locals who turned a nice profit.

Mr. Chin and Mr. Marican

Since visiting ships required various services such as fresh food, garbage removal, and even money exchange at a fair price, I was privileged to have two excellent gentlemen help me provide what the ships and their crews needed.

Mr. Chin was ethnic Chinese who dealt in jewelry, money changing, discounted lodging, and was most helpful in my dealings with local officials. Upon asking Chin how he was always able to accomplish things in dealing with police chiefs and mayors, he replied,

"I always say to them, 'never tell Mr. Chin no, tell Mr. Chin, maybe.'"

I used that approach later in life, with mixed results.

Incidentally, Thais are addressed by their first names as their surnames are nearly unpronounceable by the Occidental tongue. The "Mr." was a polite preface as was the word "Khun," which was similar in meaning to the honorary word "San" used by the Japanese.

During ship visits, Mr. Chin would arrive with a police escort and briefcases full of Thai baht (money) to be exchanged for dollars on board the ships. Chin's exchange rate beat local bank and money changer rates and he always brought along jewelry and gifts sailors could purchase before going ashore to spend all their money.

One of the most amusing sights I recall during a ship visit was Mr. Chin's mother, 60-year-old "Khun Mama," (ladies frequently held the purse strings in Thailand) climbing a steep ship's ladder with a death grip on a briefcase full of baht, while the wind whipped her skirt halfway to her head. We watched fascinated, wondering whether money or modesty would prevail. Money won out. Mama, skirt whipping, made it to the top. So did the briefcase.

Mr. Marican was ethnic Indian and a long-time ships chandler, providing all kinds of consumables needed by ships in port. If it existed in Thailand, Mr. Marican could obtain it. Chin and Marican had been friends for years, worked well together, and spoke and wrote excellent English. Being somewhat sensitive to suspicions that I may be colluding with either, or both, I made a point of assuring each ship's supply officer that I had no financial interest in either Chin's or Marican's businesses and that the ship was welcome to find a better deal anywhere they could. There were no takers. I was also careful to take no favors from either of them. On occasion, one or the other would treat me and my staff to lunch, but I was careful to reciprocate in kind.

Burma

Our Defense Attaché Office was one of the few worldwide to have received a brand-new Beechcraft Kingair twin-engine turboprop which seated eight, including two pilots, was pressurized and flew above 20,000 feet at speeds more than four miles per minute. Our military version was called a C-12A. The Beech service contract provided an on-site, full-time representative, Terry Singer, who had access to any aircraft parts he needed from the Beech factory in Wichita, Kansas. During my four-year tour, we never cancelled a flight for lack of parts or maintenance.

As I was the only attaché in our office accredited to Burma (now Myanmar), each month I flew our C-12A to Rangoon (Yangon) for several days to visit the resident U.S. Defense Attaché, Army Colonel Harry Moore, and to call on Burmese Navy officials. I also sponsored dinner parties at Harry's house for our Burmese friends.

I was favorably impressed with the Burmese peoples' command of the English language and their good feelings toward Americans. Sadly, nearly all the government buildings, while once grand, appeared rather run down and covered with vines and mold. Nearly all citizens rode buses, most of which were more run down than the buildings. The buses were a hazard, especially at night, to other vehicles and pedestrians, as they often operated with one, and sometimes, no headlights. When seats were filled, riders clung to the sides and the buses heeled well over toward the side with the most "clingers."

George and Ernie

My main Burmese Navy contact was senior captain (later Rear Admiral and Commander-in-Chief of the Burmese Navy) "George" Maung Maung Win, who was so highly regarded by the Burmese government that he represented Burma during International Law of the Sea conferences.

George was always pleasant and informative and, although usually careful not to say so, seemed to wish for the old days when the British ruled. I also frequently partied with the second senior Burmese Air Force officer, a colonel we called "Ernie." Ernie had been a British Spitfire pilot in Burma during World War II. In the 1970s, with only a few poorly maintained American T-33 jet trainers to defend Burmese airspace, Ernie said he would have traded them for Spitfires.

During our monthly dinner parties in Rangoon, our invited Burmese guests were always accompanied by an officer assigned by the Intelligence Section of the Socialist government to monitor the conversations and behavior of our guests. Although the officer was of a rank junior to our guests, as a State man he was respected. Therefore, the name of the game for us was to see how much liquor we could serve the monitor, hoping he would miss out on our probing questions and our guests' answers.

One night we hit the jackpot, the monitor being a new man not entirely comfortable in his role yet very anxious to sample some of the fine liquor to which he usually had no access. After several drinks, to which I'm sure he was not accustomed, the monitor reported that he felt ill, excused himself and left.

The minute he was out the door Ernie and George let loose with some stellar observations about the government and how things had changed since before the 1960s when Nhe Win had become president. As the party went well past the usual hour, I remained busy dashing to the bathroom where I scrawled notes about what none of us had heard said before by senior Burmese officers.

Our guests left as happy and relaxed as we'd ever seen them and DIA complimented me on my official report of the evening. Unfortunately, future State monitors were teetotalers.

American Ambassadors to Burma

During my visits to Rangoon, I often attended parties with our American ambassador to Burma who in 1976 was Maurice Bean, the first black ambassador in that part of the world. His official car was a British Checker Cab with jump seats in the rear and rollup windows between occupants and driver. Maurice, on occasion would "over enjoy" himself and after a party one night, while climbing into the back seat, entirely missed the jump seat he was aiming for, ending up undiplomatically sprawled at my feet. He took it all in good style though, eventually making it to his target with a little help from me.

Maurice's wife, Dodie, was a pleasant and outgoing lady who, as I saw it, enjoyed the assignment more than did her husband, who in 1979 was replaced by another "first," a female ambassador. Pat Byrne was a most likeable and intelligent woman who I feel convinced the Burmese that she was as acceptable as any male ambassador. I could always make Pat laugh at my outrageous sailor stories and she sometimes flew back with me to Bangkok for a few days respite from Rangoon.

L-R

Col. Harry Moore, Barbara Moore, Ambassador Maurice Bean,

Barbara VandeWater, Captain George VandeWater,

Dodie Bean, Lt. Col. Jim Rodenberg, Carol Rodenberg

Rangoon, Burma

October 1978

Air Traffic Control

While Thai air traffic controllers had good radar and were reasonably proficient, the Burmese air control system had changed little since the 1940s. Our C-12A, call sign "Spar 14," made the 400-mile flight from Bangkok to Rangoon in less than two hours, whereupon entering Burmese airspace we were greeted by British-accented controllers who gave us our landing clearance.

Although there was usually little air traffic, on one flight I was startled to be cleared to descend through thick clouds to the same altitude as another aircraft in our vicinity. As both aircraft were on the same frequency, I had been listening to its progress. Upon questioning the controller, I was not comforted by his reply.

"Our radar is inoperative, but I think you are well clear of him."

Taking matters into my own hands, I began coordinating directly with the other aircraft, a commercial airliner. Using bearings from the Rangoon navigation facilities, we broke out of the overcast well clear of each other. The Burmese controller seemed happy for the assistance.

When checking in for landing with the Rangoon air control tower, the tower's first question was always,

"Spar 14, do you have any 'reading material?'"

Reading material referred to Playboy magazine which was banned in Burma. Since we flew a diplomatic aircraft, our cargo was not examined, so we made it a point to keep the controllers happy. Tower personnel were always the first to greet us at our aircraft and were unusually helpful in expediting our air traffic clearances.

Toasts at the Chinese Embassy

On occasion, humorous incidents occurred during attaché official functions. One of note was in 1979 during the celebration by the Chinese embassy of the establishment of the People's Liberation Army, hosted by none other than Mr. Mao, accompanied as always by his trusty interpreter, Mr. Jo.

The event took place at the Chinese embassy's "Grand Room," which looked rather like a cafeteria outfitted with a few folding chairs scattered about and a large, potted plant next to each of the five tables. In full view of the guests was a swinging door to the kitchen where the main course would come on the arms of waiters dressed in drab uniforms nearly matching Mao's Mao jacket.

Before dinner could be served, protocol called for rounds of toasts to various individuals and entities important to some of us. The toasts were poured into plastic wine glasses and consisted of a clear liquor, likely 140 proof or more, called…you guessed it…a Mao Tai. It was tough to get down without gasping for breath.

I was seated at a table with my usual dinner partner, Soviet Colonel Anatoli Gouriev, the MiG pilot. Within arm's length of our table stood one of the larger potted plants appearing much in need of a drink from the water bottle that decorated the center of our table.

With our glasses constantly recharged by roving waiters, Mao, through Jo, would ring out a toast, whereupon we all sprang to our feet and downed the contents of the glass, or at least some of it. After several toasts, Mr. Jo approached our table saying that Mr. Mao requested we completely drain our glasses each toast. Although Gouriev assured Jo that we'd do better, on the next round I saw the colonel slip his Mao Tai into our potted plant and then pour water into his toasting glass. Apparently, the host also noticed.

After two more toasts, the inscrutable Mr. Mao himself approached our table and looking directly at Gouriev had Mr. Jo say,

"In the spirit of cooperation between once great allies, the Soviets and Chinese representatives will now exchange fully-charged toast glasses."

The Soviet's goose was cooked. The colonel, who had shortly before filled his wine glass with water, blanched and weakly waved his hand but was hardly able to refuse. The two then exchanged their glasses and lifted them to the next toast. While Gouriev gasped over the real stuff, Mr. Mao gave not the slightest indication that he had downed water. Staring at Gouriev for a moment, then turning his back, he walked away, inscrutable as ever, while the rest of us at the table, save the colonel, merely smirked.

Like most of us, Anatoli did not appear to enjoy the main course of "strangled" chicken, complete with attached head and feet. While I never got around to asking Mao if the potted plant at our table survived the evening's festivities, I did let Gouriev know that he needed to develop a tolerance for beverages more potent than vodka. He declined to comment.

The score that night in Bangkok… Chinese-one, Soviets-zero.

A Burma Mountain Top

Another incident occurred in 1980 which, while ending well and humorous, could well have been fatal for the ten attachés aboard a Burmese Air Force aircraft.

On rare occasions, the Burmese would host an attaché trip to various installations in Burma, such as the "Remount Station" near Mandalay where polo ponies and pack animals were bred, the former for the few idle rich, the latter for issue to soldiers who needed access to remote mountain areas unfit for even four-wheel drive vehicles.

The plan was to fly to an airstrip near Mandalay and from there via four-wheel drive vehicles to the Station. Unfortunately, that day there were low clouds hugging the mountain tops which meant our aircraft would be forced to make an instrument approach.

As we boarded our Burmese Air Force aircraft, a rickety-looking twin engine machine, I asked one of the pilots, who was enjoying his lit cigarette next to a wing filled with fuel, what navigation facility we'd be using for our approach.

"All we have there is a low-frequency radio beacon on a mountain top near the airstrip," he replied, not addressing the fact that the forecast thunderstorms would have embedded lightning which adversely affected low frequency facilities.

Turning to the British Defense Attaché, Colonel Alan Crabtree, I voiced my concern and wondered out loud,

"Do we really need to see a horse and mule farm that badly?"

Not surprisingly, in the true British spirit he replied,

"We're here, old man. We must press on."

The rest of our group, none of them pilots except me, seemed unconcerned, acting as if "What could go wrong on a flight of only 350 miles?" They were about to find out.

During the flight, I was seated on the left side of the cabin one seat behind the Indonesian Naval Attaché, Lt. Col. Oom, a rather young and excitable man. In the seat across the aisle from Oom was bespectacled Col. Crabtree, a no-nonsense officer, who 100 years prior would have been a perfect choice to command Gurkha soldiers in "In-ja," as he called it.

En route, the weather was clear above a thick overcast shrouding the mountain tops, but cumulus clouds, as forecast, were building. As we began our approach, I hoped to see breaks in the clouds but there were none. Down we went, engines at idle. Several attachés, peering out the windows, began to act nervous. I was already in that condition.

As we entered the clouds, all cabin chatter ceased. After several minutes and several thousand feet of descent, the engines suddenly went to full power and the nose of the aircraft lurched upwards…just as a huge hill loomed up from what I estimated to be 100 feet below the aircraft. I could see individual leaves on the treetops. That did it for non-pilot Oom, who erupted in a shrill, girl-like scream,

"Oh my God, we almost hit the ground. Oh my God, we almost hit the ground."

Indeed, we had, but as Oom showed no sign of winding down, Crabtree abruptly turned toward him and above the roar of the engines, shouted in his most commanding British-accented voice,

"OH, SHUT UP YOU NINNY, JUST SHUT THE HELL UP!

The tension in the cabin snapped and save for Oom and the irate Crabtree, we roared with laughter.

Climbing back above the overcast, the pilots proceeded to a clear area, as they should have done in the first place, and eventually found our airfield. During our visit to the Station, young girls presented us with flowers and lunch was served (which we hoped was beef and not Remount rejects). By the time we left the Station, the weather had cleared, allowing a much less stressful return to Rangoon. At the conclusion of the flight, even Crabtree agreed with me that the Remount Station visit was not that interesting.

With only six months left in my tour, I resolved that on my next trip to northern Burma, I'd opt for an overloaded bus, or even a Remount mule, but no more Burmese Air Force transportation. Which would have been a wise choice, as shortly after my return to the U.S., I learned of the crash of a Burmese Air Force aircraft flying in the same area under similar conditions. All aboard were lost.

Doing Business in Asia

The business world in foreign countries and even in the United States is not always as it seems. There are often confidential addenda to contracts including such things as payoffs to middlemen, or even "middlewomen." While I was not surprised, I was disappointed to see a glaring example in late 1977 involving the purchase of several patrol craft by a country I was accredited to.

Two of the final bidders were a European firm and one from the U.S. While the proposals of both companies met specifications, the U.S. company promised a better performing craft at a cheaper price, which would seem to favor the American firm. However, there was a major factor in play…unaccounted for "tea" money.

The first week of December, our embassy Commercial Officer asked if I would introduce the American representative to the appropriate naval officers who would oversee the contract award. Agreeing, I escorted the CEO of the U.S. firm to the appropriate headquarters.

Ted (whose last name I don't remember) was a giant of a man, about six feet six inches tall, and one of the most pleasant and professional businessmen I have met. As expected, we were well received and upon being seated were offered the obligatory tea and cookies.

In a concise and informative session, Ted presented his firm's updated specifications and pricing. The senior staff officer smiled politely, asked several questions and seemed genuinely impressed with the U.S. offer. He also admitted that the Americans had the best boat at the best price. After 30 minutes we departed, I with the distinct impression that the American firm would be awarded the contract. Wrong! A month went by without word of which firm had won the contract. After I'd had several queries from Ted, one evening over cocktails with a friend who was at the briefing, I inquired about the status of the contract award. My friend smiled and motioned me to a quiet spot at the bar.

"While it has not been made public," he said, "the Europeans have won the entire contract."

I was stunned.

"How could that be?" I asked. "You and I both heard your boss admit that the Americans had the best boats at the best price."

"You don't understand," he answered guardedly. "There was no upfront cash from the Americans. Your man didn't carry a large briefcase that he 'forgot' to take with him when he left the briefing, but the European rep did. While I'm not privy to the exact amount, there are rumors it was five figures in U.S. dollars, which were spread around headquarters, as appropriate."

"Tell me, my good friend," I inquired, "did you end up with a small bonus last December?"

Smiling, while ordering another round, he replied,

"So how do you think I paid for drinks tonight on my meager salary?"

I don't think it would have made a difference if Ted had known how the system worked, since I doubt that his small firm would have the cash necessary to cement such a deal. Besides, he might not have wanted to play the game.

I passed the information to Ted, who said little but was obviously disappointed. A few years later, his firm went out of business.

A Tour for a Congressman

In December 1977, Ambassador Whitehouse asked if I would be available to escort Congressman Floyd Spence (R-SC) around Bangkok, pointing our places of interest, particularly Patpong, which was the downtown area full of things of interest to visitors, especially male visitors.

"George," he said in his most charming sing-song voice, "with all your experience guiding sailors around Thailand, you'd be perfect for the job."

"Mr. Ambassador," I answered, "I'd be honored to pass on what little I know about sin city any time the Congressman is available."

"Good, I knew I could count on you, George," he answered. "In fact, I'll have my official car and my driver take you any place you want to go and wait for you at the curb."

Two days later, at the welcome aboard party for the Congressional delegation at the Ambassador's residence, I was introduced to Mr. Spence, a charming and gracious Southern gentleman, who after a second cocktail was most anxious to be off on our tour.

Decked out in casual attire, off we went in the ambassador's black Cadillac limousine. With diplomatic flags flying, we had no problem finding a curb parking place in the heart of Patpong, right in front of the "Blue Fox" bistro, where several of the resident lovelies were in the middle of a rather scintillating dance performance.

Seeming to enjoy the surroundings, the congressman graciously offered to pay for the first round of drinks from his congressional travel allowance, which if I remember correctly, was in the neighborhood of $450 per day, adequate to purchase drinks for the entire bar, plus a few trinkets for the folks back home in the Palmetto State. Somehow, I certainly don't know how, the word got around as to who we were and before we began our second round of drinks, we were mobbed by nubile ladies wishing to know us better. Mr. Spence seemed to enjoy the attention.

"George," he remarked with a smile, "this is sure different from the bars in "Foggy Bottom".

After the second, or maybe it was the third round of drinks, I recommended that we walk around and see at least several more bars, which we did, finally arriving back at the limo some two hours later.

In the car, returning to Mr. Spence's hotel suite, he turned to me and profusely thanked me for my time and the tour saying,

"George, I'm on the House Ethics Committee where we pass judgment on sin and all that stuff, so a tour like this is most important. Why how would I recognize sin unless I'd been right down there in the middle of it?"

The congressman was not re-elected in 1978 but was returned to the House during the Reagan era. I often wished I could have accepted his kind invitation to visit him in Washington. He promised he'd take me around Foggy Bottom on a Friday night, although he admitted it wouldn't measure up to Patpong.

Ambassador Whitehouse called me the next day informing me that, based upon Mr. Spence's report, I could expect to be assigned as escort to any future congressmen anxious for after dark tours. I didn't know whether to be pleased or distressed, as such a task might interfere with the many hours I usually spent each night in the embassy library researching human behavior under stressful conditions.

The First Lady Visits

In November 1979, in response to the Cambodian genocide and the influx of refugees to southern Thailand, First Lady Rosalynn Carter arrived to see what could be done to help the situation.

Initially, we were to fly Mrs. Carter to the U.N refugee camp, but the Royal Thai Air Force was adamant that they be allowed the honor. The Americans would have to settle for taking part of her Secret Service contingent in our C-12A

Shaking hands with the First Lady, I thought she was a bit distant and not thrilled about being exposed to the oppressive heat. Her Secret Service agents on the other hand were a delightful group, open and talkative, and not bothered by much of anything. We flew them from Bangkok to Songkhla near the Malaysian border with Thailand and then escorted the entire group to the U.N. camp near there.

The Cambodian refugees were in a pitiful state, having fled by boat from the murderous Khmer Rouge regime which was systematically killing off that country's middle and upper classes. After a few hours inspecting the camp, Mrs. Carter having done her duty was able to fit in some shopping in Songkhla before departing for Bangkok.

Thanking us and managing a wry smile, she handed me a set of Jimmy Carter presidential cuff links which I have yet to wear. While I liked the Secret Service agents, I felt that the rest of her delegation was less pleasant. I had been spoiled by Floyd Spence and his happy group.

Back to Vietnam

For the first time since mid-1968, on 15 January 1980 I returned to Vietnam without being fired upon by men not happy to be on the receiving end of the ten 500-pound bombs dropped from my F4 Phantom.

This time I was flying our C-12A with a delegation of congressmen led by Congressman Lester Wolff (D-NY), in my view a rather pompous and acerbic man. My copilot, who had not flown the unfriendly skies of Vietnam, was Col. Jim Diddle. Our mission was to land at Gia Lam after which the delegation would proceed downtown for talks with the Vietnamese regarding POWs and MIAs. Jim and I would remain at the airfield keeping a close eye on our airplane.

The flight itself was without incident, the Vietnamese air controllers speaking passable English and providing vectors for landing. No MiGs were sighted. Parking before a welcoming committee of sorts, the first glitch occurred. Popping open the cabin door, our enlisted crewman bounded down the steps only to be immediately recalled by one of Mr. Wolff's aides who informed all within hearing that the congressman would be the first to deplane in front of the arriving cameramen.

Ten minutes later, all was ready, and the smiling congressman descended the steps first, followed by lesser members of the delegation, all of whom clambered into a few non-descript vehicles and departed the airport for central Hanoi.

Diddle and I looked at each other, relieved to be on our own for a few hours, despite being escorted by a surly Vietnamese guard armed with an AK-47 which looked to be locked and loaded. Interestingly, the guard spoke some English and probably understood much more.

Not far from our parked aircraft was a yellow fuel truck which looked to be a "liberated" U.S. model, now pock-marked with shrapnel damage. Walking to the truck, I turned to the guard pointing to the damage and asked what had happened to the vehicle.

"Americans," our escort mumbled, "maybe you."

Grimacing, I shook my head and said,

"Not me. 'I'm a great pilot and I would have blown up the whole truck."

This unhinged the soldier who apparently understood what I said. Shaking his rifle at me, he blustered,

"Shut up, you American air pirate!"

I took his advice and said nothing further, not anxious to be the last American casualty of the Vietnam war some seventeen years after the war ended, and for not a good enough reason.

Diddle, meanwhile, had become fascinated with the bricks which made up the taxiway we were parked on. Bending over, he attempted to pry one up, torching off an already upset soldier who pointed the barrel of his weapon six inches from Jim's head and shouted,

"No do, no do!"

Diddle looked up and said,

"My father-in-law collects bricks," which was probably not understood by our guard, or in any event would not have been approved.

Standing between the two, I asked loudly,

"Jim, are you prepared to have your brains blown out for this worthless brick? This guy is likely to shoot you for stealing the people's property."

Diddle snapped back to reality and stood up without the brick. Anxious to defuse the situation, I suggested to our guard, by pointing, that we walk over to a wire fence which separated the airfield from a small village. At the fence stood a very pretty young girl, outfitted in a conical hat and black pajamas, holding a basket containing something wrapped in banana leaves. Oddly, the guard did not object, possibly having in mind that we might buy something with American dollars, some of which he might claim as a finder's fee.

Young as she was, the girl acted as if doing business with foreigners was part of her day's work. As I held out my cash, the girl pointed to a five-dollar bill and handed me two banana leaves filled with brown rice and two beverages of some kind in Coke bottles with corks sticking from the tops. Thinking it to be a bargain and with no prospects for lunch, I agreed, whereupon the guard smiled, pointed first to the girl and then to himself and said in clear English, "Sister." It wasn't a great lunch, but the tension between us seemed to ease.

For the next hour we moved about the taxiway and examined, among other things, an old control tower, also with shrapnel damage. I took care to make no comment. Diddle now seemed to interpret the guard's attitude as becoming permissive and he had begun looking at the taxiway bricks again.

"Jim," I warned, "I know what you're thinking, but let's behave for the next few minutes and return home with two pilots, both of us alive."

He remained unconvinced, however, later saying that he wished he'd offered our escort money for bricks. I heartedly disagreed then and I still do.

Some two hours after leaving, the motorcade returned and deposited our delegation, none of whom looked happy. Smiling at our new "best friend" escort, who returned the smile, Diddle and I climbed aboard for an uneventful return to Bangkok.

Leaving Vietnam airspace, I looked back wondering what I'd do if a SAM missile were to be fired at our defenseless C-12A. While it certainly was no F4, I might just be able to pull off a maneuver causing the missile to miss. How delightful, I thought, to see Mr. Wolff's reaction…with no onboard cameramen to record his bravery…or lack thereof.

Despite favorable press coverage back home in New York, Congressman Wolff was not re-elected to the House in 1980.

Chapter Nine
Avoiding Washington, Again

In October 1980, Defense Intelligence Agency notified me that they would ask the Navy to order me to Washington, D.C. to run their European desk. While appreciative of their confidence, I wanted nothing to do with Washington or the Pentagon. Asking my detailer what other possibilities there were, he replied,

"How about a Naval Reserve Officers Training Corps unit?"

Relieved that I'd be spared Washington duty and without asking where I'd be assigned, I gladly accepted.

In five days, I had message orders to NROTC Prairie View A&M, which surprised me as I'd never heard of it before. Ambassador Abramowitz, having seen the orders (ambassadors see all message traffic) called to ask if I knew what I had signed up for.

"Prairie View is a small college with an even smaller NROTC unit entirely beneath your capabilities," he said. "Let's see if I can get you a more challenging job."

In three more days, I had orders to the University of Texas in Austin, a significant step up. For this and other things, I will be forever in debt to Ambassador Abramowitz.

The downside of my new assignment was that we'd be leaving Thailand and all the perquisites that Barbara and I had enjoyed for four years. No longer would I be greeted at the front door by our maid, Deng, as she exchanged an ice-cold martini for my briefcase. Nor would we have our chef, Jerry, prepare gourmet meals on short notice for our many guests. No more flying about Southeast Asia in an airplane that I had come to view as my personal transportation. We would be leaving Thai and Burmese military and civilian friends we had cultivated over the years and the twenty-six members of the Military Attaché Corps of Thailand, of which I was by then the dean. How would Colonel Gouriev do without my frequent needling? And the inscrutable Mr. Mao? Would he ever admit being an officer in the Peoples' Army?

By letter I briefed my relief, Captain Larry Sharpe, about the good things he could look forward to. We would have adequate time for a smooth handover of duties and introductions to the people he would be working closely with. It all worked out very nicely and Mr. Chin and Mr. Marican had a new boss.

George
Bangkok, Thailand
May 1980

Military Attache Plaque
November 1980

Back to the States

In early December 1980, Barbara and I, with our daughter, Kathy, (Philip had returned to California earlier) departed Bangkok, seen off by dozens of our friends at the VIP lounge at Don Muang airport. Despite our best intentions to return, we would not see Thailand again.

By early January 1981, we had bought a house in Georgetown, Texas, some twenty miles north of Austin and I had met my NROTC staff and our students. The staff was a good one, comprised of Navy officer instructors and a Marine major who was the contact point for those who would become Marine officers. The several Navy senior petty officers and civilian secretaries were efficient and pleasant to work with. Our students were young, very young, or so it seemed – I who had been long away from college campuses, but they were enthusiastic and motivated to become Navy and Marine officers.

Unfortunately, I found most of the university professors decidedly anti-military. With the Vietnam experience still fresh in the minds of academia, they were at best distant and when engaged in conversation seemed unwilling to discuss anything other than their own area of academic expertise. Most were distressed to learn that upon my arrival I was designated a full professor, something they had struggled for years to attain. They were also chagrined to learn that I was paid considerably more than most of them and I was certain that some coveted the very nice office spaces occupied by my unit.

An outstanding exception to the anti-military bias on campus was pretty and personable Malinda Wilson who organized and supervised the university's registration sessions each semester and was most valuable in assisting our young enlisted personnel on their way to becoming officers. Only slightly older than our young men, she had the educational qualifications and the no-nonsense attitude to ensure their success in what was a very different environment than ground combat. Thanks to her help, every one of our enlisted Marines became officers during my time there. To this day, Malinda remains a close family friend.

Our NROTC was in constant competition with the Army and the Air Force ROTC units for promising students. We even went so far as to mount charm offenses designed to poach the more valuable ones, offering them choice billets in aviation and submarines and, in fact, succeeding to the point where there were official protests made to me by the commanding officers of the other units. I denied such intent, noting that since we had the most to offer, one couldn't blame students for jumping to the Navy ship.

Our Marine officer instructor was Major Chuck Armstrong, a sturdy, bright, and charming individual who in the early 1980s set a world record of 1435 pull-ups in a single session of less than five hours. The students of all three ROTCs were impressed. A native Texan, Chuck organized a relay run from Austin to the Alamo in San Antonio carrying a Texas flag celebrating the 145th anniversary of the battle there. Chuck went on to publish numerous articles on the military and authored several physical fitness programs for men and women. He was one of a kind who contributed greatly to our unit's success.

Our NROTC summer cruises were a draw for students. Rather than slog around in the mud with an Army unit or fly about in an Air Force transport plane, our students went to sea in destroyers, submarines, or aircraft carriers while some of the more vigorous young men had the opportunity to spend time with Navy SEALS undergoing training at Coronado, California. Through good public relations and a hard-working staff, we were able to increase our student count by 18% during the thirty months I was there.

Virginia Tech

In the spring of 1983, I was offered the opportunity to open a new NROTC unit at Virginia Tech in Blacksburg, Virginia. While office space and logistics would be in place, I would be tasked with developing a student body in competition with long established Army and Air Force units. I jumped at the chance, not only anxious to start a new unit, but to trade the busy city life of Austin for Blacksburg. Our unit was welcomed at Virginia Tech, where the university administrators and professors seemed comfortable with the military presence, probably because of the long tradition of the Corps of Cadets there.

While summer and fall featured agreeable weather to go with the beautiful mountain scenery, the winters in the Blue Ridge mountains were harsher than I was used to. One Sunday in January 1985, I watched with disbelief as the thermometer outside our kitchen window dipped to 25 degrees below zero. The next morning, my Honda sedan's shifting gear felt as if it were stuck in rapidly curing cement. The wind chill factor was 40 below and I was pleased that it was to be my last winter in Blacksburg.

Kathy and Barbara
Encinitas, California
August 1985

George
Thailand's Order of the White Elephant
Blacksburg, Virginia
June 1985

Virginia Tech was unique in that it had a large cadet corps which had the potential to be a good source of students interested in a military career. Commandant of cadets was retired Lt. Gen. "Bones" Marshall, an Air Force veteran. We got along, but not as well as I would have liked, as Bones was primarily interested in building his cadet corps and not necessarily in providing candidates for any ROTC unit.

Our NROTC was at the leading edge of a program wherein sailboats, confiscated by the Coast Guard for smuggling, were provided free of charge to Navy ROTC units able to take advantage of a sailing program. We obtained a 43-foot sailboat that had been apprehended trying to smuggle marijuana into Charleston harbor one night in 1982.

San Diego State University
From Left: Philip, George, Kathy,
Jason, Barbara
June 1986

"Esprit de Corps" was nicely set up for cruising and for instructing midshipmen in seamanship. The only downside for a strait-laced Navy captain was that when the bow section got damp, which it frequently did, the smell of marijuana was quite noticeable. Other than that, the boat was a great cruising platform.

Each weekend we would load up a van with midshipman and drive to Charleston for two days of sailing and living aboard. Eating dinner while anchored off the Battery in downtown Charleston was a pleasant experience not available to the Army and Air Force units.

While I enjoyed certain aspects of training young men and women to become Navy and Marine officers, I greatly missed my days of flying, going to sea in aircraft carriers and, most of all, the good life and challenges of four years working for DIA in Southeast Asia. I was ready to retire.

Chapter Ten
The Civilian World

In June 1985, we departed Blacksburg for retirement in Encinitas, California. Having purchased a 1962 Mooney, a small four-place airplane, for a bargain price, I planned to show Barbara the U.S. from the air. I also would continue as an instructor in sailplanes which I had begun in Texas in 1981. By 1986, having finished building our retirement home, I was becoming bored. A two month-vacation in Europe was helpful, but I still craved dealing with people and aviation.

Aviation Recruiting

In May 1987 I responded to a recruitment ad from Spartan School of Aeronautics and was interviewed by Spartan representatives Terry Harrison and Steve Waggoner. There were three other candidates included in the group interview, one who appeared to struggle to stay awake while another reeked of alcohol. The third, Stan Swift, appeared to be more competitive, stating that he had held many sales jobs and was skilled in dealing with people.

I frankly noted that I had never held a sales position, but felt qualified to discuss aviation on any level and had managed people in small and large units over the last 30 years. Terry, who was CEO of Spartan, appeared sold on me, but Steve held out for Stan, the man with the sales experience. Terry solved the dilemma by hiring both of us.

In the first three months, I recruited 30 students while Stan, no matter how hard he worked, recruited none. Terry was vindicated. Over the years, Steve and I have become the best of friends, despite my occasional reference to his "lapse" in good judgment. Steve just smiles and nods his head.

After three months with Spartan, I was offered the job as director of their flight school, a position which paid little with a staff I judged to be inept. During my interview of the flight school staff members, I asked some very penetrating questions which alarmed several to the point where they relayed to the school president that I would be a tyrant and impossible to work for. I agreed that at least the latter would be true, as I planned to immediately fire the complainers. Alarmed, the president withdrew his offer and in turn, I withdrew from Spartan, convinced that the school was on a downhill trend.

Automobile Sales

Still casting about for something to do, in early 1990 I answered another advertisement for a sales position, this time for automobiles. In the late 1940s, my dad had been a Dodge-Plymouth dealer and I had been fascinated by the interplay between salesmen and customers. Those, of course, were the days when the pent-up demand for new cars made customers easy pickings for salesmen.

Times had changed, however, and car salesmen in 1990 were rather predatory. As a newly minted Hyundai salesman, I was amazed at the machinations used to entrap customers. One case in point was the arrival on a bus of a young Marine E-3 from nearby Camp Pendleton who stepped off the bus with his wife holding the hand of a young child and obviously expecting another. I watched in dismay as that poor couple indebted themselves for the next five years, owing nearly $10,000 for a vehicle that listed for $5000. Although I had enjoyed considerable success in selling that fine little car with the full-size spare tire, that incident triggered my resignation. I'd go next door to the Cadillac agency which surely would have a different view of customers who had many options. Wrong.

After one month selling Cadillacs, the sales manager called me aside pointing out that he was unhappy with my performance.

"Why was that?" I asked as I had sold eight cars already.

"George," he said, "you're doing it all wrong. You get those old people gabbing over a cup of coffee, learn all about their backgrounds and make friends. Get the old fuds into their new car and off our lot before they have a heart attack and die."

I thanked the manager for his insight and said I'd return in the morning to pick up the commissions owed me for my sales that week. That was the end of automobile sales for me.

George and Philip
Lifesaving Medal
Encinitas, California
May 1991

Barbara and Jason
Encinitas, California
May 1991

Chapter Eleven
Pipeline Patrol

My left arm jerks involuntarily, seared for what must be the tenth time in as many minutes by a shoulder harness buckle baked painfully hot in the blazing heat of the June 1996 noonday sun. I can't release the flight controls for even a second, buffeted as I am by savage thermals boiling up from the New Mexico desert 500 feet below my Mooney. Mindful of the hazards of heat exhaustion in a cockpit temperature of over 100 degrees, I try for a gulp of water from my two-quart bottle. Wham! Another tremendous lifting jolt slams the bottle to my lap, unopened. This is ceasing to be fun, but maybe it's just because I'm getting old and inflexible after forty-six years of flying and well past my sixty-second birthday.

Counting the thirty-minute fuel stop in Casa Grande, Arizona, it's been six hours since I lifted off from Palomar airport on the coast north of San Diego, just as the sun rose over the Imperial Valley's Salton Sea.

Joining my patrol route at Niland, California, I'd rounded the turn at Imperial and lined up on the taxiway south of Navy El Centro's runway 26, the same runway that in mid-March 1958 I'd landed my FJ-3 Fury jet after my engine had seized at 200 feet above the ground. Too low to eject, I can still hear the grinding sound as I slid to a halt half-way down the runway, the underwing missile rails absorbing nearly all the damage. Awarded membership in the Commander Naval Air Forces Pacific's "Old Pro Club" at age 26 for my minimal damage feat, I must admit to being in the right place at the right time, or at least the right place.

Luck. It's odd how often luck has played a part in my aviation career. Luck and timing, as we naval aviators were fond of saying, trump skill and cunning, or so it seems. As on my approach to the traffic pattern at George Air Force Base in the summer of 1956 when I luckily looked left from my right-hand turn in time to spot four F-100s on a collision course with me and my wingman, which the tower had cleared into the pattern in front of me.

Timing. As in the case of the Rockwell Commander aircraft that I sometimes flew on my patrols. In August 1996, just two flight hours after I returned the aircraft to Phoenix, the engine suffered a massive failure at low altitude over the southwestern Arizona desert, killing all three occupants in the ensuing crash into rough terrain. Good luck and timing for me, but not for the crew in the Rockwell.

Yet again luck and timing on my patrol north of El Paso in June 2002 when I glanced up to see an aircraft on a collision course, totally unaware of my presence. Had I not moved 50 feet to the north a few seconds earlier, attempting to read a small sign on a Mexican food factory, we would have collided at an altitude too low for either of us to have survived. Sometimes curiosity is a good thing.

And how about in the fall of 1957 when I turned down a flight with a squadron mate in a TV-2 jet trainer at Navy North Island? And I never, ever, turned down an opportunity to add to my flight hours…except this one time. The aircraft with my two friends, Curts and Downing onboard, experienced complete engine failure just after lift-off from runway 29. Too low to eject, both pilots died in the crash into San Diego Bay.

On this June day in 1996, as usual, I'm flying alone except for my four toy ducks, some sandwiches, my water bottle, and a cooler with a short-lived bag of ice. In the seat to my right are folders of pipeline route strip charts depicting every foot of the over 1000-mile route, along with the locations and names of some 220 rectifiers which provide cathodic protection for the metal pipeline. My 1962 Mooney M20C's 180 horsepower Lycoming engine is turning at 1900 rpm which, with 19 inches of manifold pressure, gives me a ground speed of 120 mph at a fuel flow of 6 gallons per hour.

Of the several types of patrol aircraft I have flown, my Mooney is the most efficient, which is important when one is paid by the number of pipeline miles flown. Now, in the trackless desert with few distractions, my mind revisits the time when the idea of flying a pipeline patrol first occurred to me.

A Pipeline Patrol Opportunity

By early 1991, after flying all over the U.S. with Barbara for six years, it dawned on me that owning even a small private airplane was a rich man's game. Adding up routine maintenance, annual inspections, insurance, tie-down fees, plus fuel and oil, I was spending nearly $10,000 a year. While I disliked travel by airlines, that amount would buy numerous cross-country trips at triple the speed of my 150 mph Mooney. What I really needed was to fly for pay.

The answer appeared that spring in the form of a rather shabby-looking Piper Super Cub tied down at a local airport with "Patrol" in large letters emblazoned on the bottom of one wing. The aircraft was owned by Union Flights of Sacramento, California and was flown on a weekly pipeline patrol between San Diego and El Paso, Texas.

I called Union Flights, learning from the Chief Pilot that they not only had two pilots, but several applications for the job, even though the pay was only $10 a flight hour and $60 a day per diem. I was welcome to submit a resume, he said, but there were highly qualified applicants ahead of me, so I shouldn't get my hopes up. I pointed out that I had 40 years of flight experience in many types of military and civilian aircraft, along with a spotless record of no accidents, incidents, or flight violations in over 8000 flight hours. I noted that I was familiar with the route between San Diego and El Paso, having flown it many times in my own aircraft. They would call me, the Chief Pilot said, if they needed me.

Meanwhile, the Cub continued its weekly patrols piloted by a young mechanic hired more for his skill with a wrench than for his flying abilities. The company, being cost-conscious, preferred a pilot who was also an FAA licensed aircraft mechanic. Fred, as we'll call him, was their first choice…for a while.

In late May, near Lordsburg, New Mexico, Fred lost control of his machine while "checking out" an antelope herd, demolishing the Cub and very nearly himself. After regaining his senses, such as they were, Fred dragged himself two miles to Interstate 10, oozing blood from a head wound and a broken ankle. Finally, after being passed by numerous suspicious motorists, he managed to convince one that he "really, really," needed a lift to town.

"We wondered where he went," said the pipeline company operator responsible for keeping track of the patrol pilot.

And so exited Fred who, if he has ceased flying, may still be limping about California.

With an equally shabby replacement Cub online, the company's next choice was Fred's backup pilot, a Neanderthal type fellow with a shaggy beard and a prodigious stomach who, hopefully, was more skilled at flying than was his predecessor. With the company's stable of pilots now reduced to one, Bart, as we'll call him, needed a backup pilot.

Late one evening the Chief Pilot called. He'd been sifting through the "many" resumes and asked if I was still interested. Wondering what had become of the many applicants ahead of me, but not wishing to rock the boat, I agreed to sign on over the phone and was hired, sight unseen. The good news was that I'd be getting paid for plenty of flight time. The bad news was that Bart would be my checkout pilot.

I had met Bart at a small airport east of San Diego where I instructed in sailplanes and gave passengers sightseeing rides. He was one of the glider tow plane pilots and nearly perfect for the job, his appearance matching the tattered Piper Pawnee tow planes. He flew with his beard blowing in the slipstream and his stomach overhanging his filthy jeans, soaked in what I hoped was oil and grease from the brace of Harley motorcycles he worked on when not flying the pipeline or towing gliders. Bart also drove a big-rig fuel truck to make ends meet. He looked like what I thought a big-rig driver should look like, but then I didn't know any big-rig drivers, so apologies may be in order.

Thunderstorms and Cloud Banks

Bart and I had our first and very nearly our last flight together in July 1991. My first doubts regarding his aviation knowledge and common sense surfaced on our leg from Yuma to Phoenix where a gigantic afternoon thunderstorm blocked our path. With no intercom in the Cub, we were reduced to shoulder jabbing and shouting above the engine's roar as our primary communication, supplemented if time allowed with notes passed back and forth. As we approached the huge dust cloud in front of the storm, I began "communicating" with Bart from the back seat with a series of forceful jabs and shouts. I couldn't believe he was planning to enter that boiling cauldron, but only upon me opening the fold down cabin door and making like I was about to step out did Bart get the message to steer clear.

The next incident on our return route two days later convinced me that Bart had even less sense than Fred and that with him in charge in the front seat (the rear stick was removed to make more room for the pilot seated there to fold out route charts) my aviation luck could well run out.

Passing Temecula, California, southbound along Interstate 15 on our last leg to our home airport of Oceanside, we could see towering clouds covering the hilly terrain, the remnants of a rare tropical storm in the San Diego area. Bart appeared unfazed and headed directly at the cloud bank. This time, rather than using our tried and true shoulder jab system, I whacked Bart hard on the back of his sweaty neck, accompanied by my shout likely audible on the highway below.

"What are you doing, you idiot?" I politely inquired. "Can't you see we're flying straight into a cloud bank?"

Bart looked back at me confused, offering his opinion that it was probably "just a thin cloud and clear on the other side." The problem was that not only did the Cub lack the instruments necessary for instrument flight, even if it was so equipped, Bart was not qualified to fly on instruments. Besides, we had no clearance from air traffic control to fly under instrument conditions.

Just as the ground began to disappear and likely because of the bludgeoning he was taking, Bart got the picture and reversed course. After more shouted advice from the back seat, we finally found a clear path home via the San Luis Rey riverbed.

Bart and I were finished. As we deplaned, the silence between us was finally broken by Bart's lame comment about the unusual weather, which was promptly answered by uncivil remarks from me regarding his abject stupidity and complete lack of good judgement.

"How on earth can you be so dumb as to try to fly through a thunderstorm and then through clouds masking a hilltop?" I asked.

He had no answer.

"Look, I said, "I've flown for 40 years with thousands of accident-free hours. I've made it through night carrier landings in the foulest of weather, been shot at many times over Vietnam and now, twice, you've tried your level best to make my wife a widow. I don't appreciate that and as soon as I can get to a phone, I'll inform Union Flights that we've had our first and last flight together and the reasons why."

Bart blanched and apologized profusely. If I'd give him another chance, he'd swear never to do anything foolish again. And, he desperately needed the income. Looking at his forlorn face, I felt sorry for him and relented. We'd meet again the next Monday, provided he understood that I was in charge and he would abide by my rules and judgement. He agreed, fervently thanking me and shaking my hand. For several minutes after Bart walked away, I wondered if I had made the right decision. We'd find out starting the next week.

Bart Departs

Things improved somewhat on our next flight. Bart was a whiz on the pipeline. He knew the 1000-mile route by heart and each of the many rectifiers by name and location. Too bad he was so rough cut and during hot weather it would be nice if he would dab on some deodorant since, with him in the front seat, the breeze blew the scent of his ripe corpus into my highly sensitive nostrils.

Also, Bart's jokes were the rankest I'd ever heard. He persisted in telling the worst of them to the sweet young girls attending the desks at our fuel stops, causing them to blush and me to explode in irritation. Bart, forty years old, had never married and dated only biker girls. I could see why he was single.

While my aviation luck continued, Bart's ran out in August 1991 on a solo patrol through the Banning Pass near Palm Springs. He had spotted an errant trailer park resident loading a wheelbarrow with dirt from the pipeline right of way, an immediate problem only if the dirt hijacker was equipped with a power tool that extended down eight feet to the twenty-inch line with over 1000 pounds of pressure transferring fuel products from Los Angeles to Phoenix.

Bart, diligent as he was, circled the miscreant and announced over the Cub's loud-speaker system,

"Don't excavate the pipeline, it's dangerous."

Unfortunately, the message was received on the ground as, "EVACUATE the pipeline, it's DANGEROUS." Unbeknownst to Bart, there had been a major explosion and fire at that very site a few years prior when a bulldozer had hit and ruptured the pipeline, which was well remembered by the park's residents. Such an announcement from a plane marked "Patrol" was taken to mean flee the area…pronto. The ensuing fiasco resulting from frantic evacuees smashing into each other heading to the open highway had to be quelled by sheriff's deputies. When the dust cleared, the pipeline company was presented with a substantial bill for vehicular damage and the deputies' time spent calming the residents. Bart was done.

The day following Bart's incident, about which I knew nothing, I received a rather cryptic call from the pipeline company's Tucson office asking if Bart broke his leg would I be ready to take over? I, of course, assured the company executive that I was indeed capable and ready. Seeming satisfied with my answer the call ended with his cheery, "Have a good day." I remained puzzled, not imagining any activity Bart could undertake, other than flying into a thunderstorm or cloud-covered hill or falling off one of his Harleys, that would result in a broken leg.

The next day, the riddle was solved in a phone call from Bart who dejectedly informed me that,

"Well, you've got the job. I've just been fired."

He went on to explain that the pipeline company had told Union Flights to "fire that pilot" and cared not for any explanations. While I believed Bart, there was no going back. In just over a month I had gone from backup pilot to primary pilot. Despite feeling sorry for Bart, I was happy to have his job. During the next few months, we stayed in contact, Bart finally landing a job with the San Diego County Sheriff's maintenance department greasing police cars. Along with his tow pilot job, he said he was getting by, but that he missed his pipeline patrol flights. I didn't comment.

My mind returns to the patchwork desert floor beneath the blunt nose of my Mooney, dull-tan sand bordering intense green circles where center pivot irrigation systems nourish soils that can grow anything. It's well past three o'clock and the thermals have slackened somewhat as I approach El Paso where I'll spend that night with my mother, another job benefit, since I see her nearly every week. Under tower control, I follow my route across the approach end of dual runways 26L and 26R, reverse course over downtown and prepare to land after nearly eight flying hours.

The sun is directly in my eyes and fierce during my approach to a runway nearly two miles long. I park at Cutter Aviation, tie down my aircraft and depart for the night. Next morning, well before dawn, I'll depart for Deming, New Mexico where I'll fuel up at Desert Aviation, operated by Bob Benavidez, my friend and my eventual replacement.

The Super Cub

On 2 September 1991, I flew my first solo pipeline patrol from San Diego to El Paso in an airplane that had been flying as many years as I had, a 1954 Piper Super Cub PA-18, known to the Federal Aviation Administration as N82182. My call sign was Union 14, which I used with FAA facilities. The controllers knew me and my route and went out of their way to clear me through heavily traveled airspace at my usual speed of 80 knots. Except over highly populated areas where I maintained 1000 feet, my patrol altitude was 500 feet or sometimes less if I became interested in an item on the ground, such as equipment and personnel working on or near the pipeline right of way.

The Cub had nearly 16,000 hours on its airframe which was showing signs of wear and tear. The fabric covering the fuselage and wings, even after having been replaced numerous times, had a few patches and the windshield and cockpit glass had several deep scratches. Union Flights referred to it as a "working" aircraft, not a showpiece, which seemed like a fair assessment.

The Lycoming 150-horsepower engine had only 1200 hours since overhaul and could be counted upon to start and run smoothly in any weather. The wheel brakes were activated by small square pedals, one on each side of the cockpit a few inches aft of the rudder pedals. The rudder pedals themselves were small bars an inch in diameter and wide enough for the average foot. It was an awkward arrangement compared to rudder pedal-mounted toe brakes and required considerable dexterity with one's feet during the taxi and landing phases of flight.

The Cub was responsive and reasonably light on the controls. It was easy to fly, although like most tailwheel configured aircraft, it demanded attention during landings. There was a single VHF radio to communicate with FAA agencies and a company radio for communication with pipeline personnel. My pipeline strip charts were contained in several three-ring notebooks which were tied down in the rear seat, along with my cooler. A knee pad was strapped to my right thigh which listed radio frequencies for the different agencies and a place to record my notes. At every fuel stop, I would report my findings to a pipeline company representative and at the completion of each patrol I submitted a comprehensive written report. I was supplied a Union Flights company credit card for fuel, oil, and tie down charges at my overnight stops.

Depending upon the weather, my usual itinerary included fuel stops at Corona, California, Yuma and Tucson, Arizona, Deming, New Mexico and El Paso, Texas. With 36 gallons of fuel and a burn rate of about 7 gallons an hour, I was never low on fuel. With the engine's roar and the blast of air through the cockpit, the cabin was noisy, necessitating a high-grade aviation headset for external communications and hearing preservation. The aircraft had no intercom. A cockpit heater helped in cold weather but there was no cure for summer temperatures exceeding 100 degrees and there was no help from outside air flow which was like a blast furnace.

A typical patrol week began on Monday at 4:00 a.m. when I had a hearty breakfast prepared by Barbara, who also loaded my cooler with ice, sandwiches, snacks, and water. I was airborne as soon as it was light enough to see the ground and concluded flying each day by sundown. After two nights on the road and 22 flight hours, I arrived home. The rest of the week I spent doing paperwork, cleaning and maintaining the aircraft and figuring the optimum weather window for the next week's patrol. All in all, I spent as much time working on ground-related tasks as I did flying the Cub , but I was happy to be paid for a unique and enjoyable job which, the truth be known, I would have done for free.

I've always talked to myself when alone, no matter what I was doing, but I developed self-conversation to a high degree during my long aerial patrols. I commented out loud about what I saw, heard, and what I thought, congratulating myself on a good maneuver and criticizing myself for a poorly executed one. I also conversed with my four toy ducks I carried with me, who merely stared up at me.

What I liked most about pipeline patrol was how different it was from my previous flying. Other than occasionally flying at low altitude in sailplanes, most of my flying had been at high speeds and high altitudes. Pipeline patrol was low and slow and, in many places, close to sagebrush, jack rabbits, coyotes, farmers working their fields, and car and truck traffic whose drivers stared up at the large letters on the bottom of one wing reading: "Patrol." Some drivers immediately slowed down, others did not.

In eastern New Mexico and west Texas there were numerous red tail hawk nests perched on the cross members of power lines where, as I flew by, I could count heads of the chicks looking up at me. Herds of antelope, at first skittish, eventually accepted my Cub as a non-threat, merely glancing up at their weekly visitor. I often saw small bands of wild horses on an Indian reservation south of Phoenix kicking up clouds of dust visible from miles away. One day, I orbited for ten minutes over two bands watching one stallion attempting to steal another's mares. I often saw golden eagles and red tail hawks diving on rabbits and ground squirrels.

One very unusual sight appeared in the summer of 1992 near Buckeye, Arizona in the form of a naked woman cooling off in an irrigation ditch alongside the pipeline right of way. Contrary to my expectations, rather than duck under the water, she popped almost all the way out, smiling and waving to me. Thereafter, I looked in vain each time I flew the route, but I never saw her again. It's possible she was arrested for indecent exposure.

One sport I particularly enjoyed was making low-level runs over pipeline company trucks driving along the right of way. Upon spotting the truck, I would descend to a very low level trying to startle the driver as I swept by overhead, rocking my wings. Usually, I received a radio call from the occupant claiming he had seen me and really wasn't startled at all, but I always suspected otherwise. I knew the names of the "line riders" along the entire route and often conversed with them by radio and phone. They were friendly and professional and rode with me on occasion so they could see the line from my perspective. During my nineteen years of patrol, some line riders retired and some changed locations. I will always miss our frequent chats.

Chapter Twelve
Hiatus and a New Opportunity

In September 1992, Union Flights informed me that they had lost the contract for the San Diego to El Paso pipeline route and that my last patrol would be at the end of October. I was greatly disappointed. Having logged almost 1300 hours in the Cub on 60 patrols over 15 months, my fun was coming to an end.

In November, I returned N82182 to Union Flights in Sacramento, meeting for the first time the chief pilot who had hired me over the phone. The contract, I was told, had been awarded to a start-up company headed by Mike Dellas, an airline pilot based in Phoenix.

Hoping for a job with Mike, I sent him a letter stating my qualifications and experience and offered to fly the line for him or assist in some other way. Thanking me, Mike noted that he had hired several young flight instructors anxious to build their flight hours. He'd call me if I was needed. As it turned out, I was needed almost immediately.

In late December, Mike called lamenting the fact that one of his flight instructors was weathered in at Banning, just west of Palm Springs, California where the wind was blowing at near hurricane velocity (which was not unusual for that time of year during Santa Ana weather conditions). His man wanted out of the patrol business, "right now," so would I be interested in not only completing that patrol but in taking over the route from San Diego to Yuma. I quickly agreed, noting that I'd be flying the Mooney aircraft I had purchased in 1984, which was far faster and more efficient than the Cessna aircraft his pilots were flying.

My only request was that I be permitted to fly the entire route from San Diego to El Paso at least once per month, to which Mike readily agreed. Confident that his inexperienced pilots would make a mistake, I now hoped for an opportunity to take over the whole route on a full-time basis.

The Whole Enchilada

In January 1993 that opportunity arose. While at Yuma on my once monthly run to El Paso, during my check in with the Phoenix station, the operator informed me that his supervisor was extremely unhappy that I had missed a major threat to the pipeline in the Maricopa area the week prior and wanted to talk to me. When I informed the supervisor that I had not flown the segment he referred to during the last three weeks, he apologized noting, however, that he would be calling the patrol company with an official complaint. Hoping to give Mike a heads up, I called and told him the story. After a few moments of silence, he abruptly said,

"George, I've had it with my guys, you've got the entire route, starting today."

I was elated, not only to be back on my beloved route, but that I now had a way to put my airplane to work, with all the associated tax and business benefits. I was now a pipeline patrol subcontractor, quite a step up from line pilot, with much better profit possibilities. Mike would pay me by pipeline miles flown which, even considering that I would be paying fuel and maintenance expenses, was a substantial increase in income. I couldn't have been happier. But then, an even better opportunity appeared.

By July 1993, Dellas decided that administering the pipeline patrol contract he held was not much fun, nor did it spin off the profits he expected, so he sold the contract to Pete Lown, CEO of his own startup company, Copperstate Aviation, also based in Phoenix at Falcon Field. Pete assured me that I would continue to fly the entire route with the proviso that I occasionally fly his company aircraft, a Rockwell Commander 112 and a Beechcraft 23 Sundowner. I could leave my Mooney at one of his tiedown spaces at Falcon field at no charge.

As the pipeline patrol contract was a small segment of Copperstate's aviation business and I was the only one of his pilots qualified to fly the line, Pete offered to transfer the entire contract to me at no fee.

I was delighted to accept his offer and, since Santa Fe Pacific (later Kinder Morgan) had no objections, on 1 January 1996 my company, Prime Air Services, officially took over from Copperstate. I was now a prime contractor and would personally deal with pipeline officials on contract pricing and services. My yearly increases in price per pipeline mile immediately proved quite profitable for me. I realized excellent tax write-offs and I finally had a full-time job for my Mooney. I had reached what I considered the pinnacle of corporate aviation.

A Dishonest Employee

In early 1996, I hired a backup patrol pilot, we'll call him Herb, a flight instructor based in Long Beach, California. Herb was a quick learner and had access to a rental Cessna 172 which he flew once a month over the entire route. He was interested in building flight time and someday taking over from me. Herb did well until greed raised its ugly head.

In the spring of 1996, a pipeline company supervisor called me saying that he was receiving written reports from Herb which missed some obvious ground excavation threats to the pipeline and that his reports did not differ from mine the week before. When I questioned Herb, he expressed amazement, saying that there must be a "misunderstanding." As it turned out, Herb would spend the night in Willcox, Arizona. Then, rather than fly the segment between Willcox and El Paso before heading back to the west, he would depart westbound from Willcox, saving fuel and rental fees on his rented aircraft but cheating the company which paid for a route segment not flown.

I was highly embarrassed and assured the supervisor I would fix the problem. Which I did by firing Herb when he was unable to convince me he was not cheating. He refused to take the polygraph test I suggested, continuing with the lame excuse that it was all a misunderstanding. I never saw nor heard from him again.

My next backup pilot, Bob Benavidez, was a cut far above Herb. He was an experienced aviator and a competent mechanic who ran Desert Aviation, a fixed base operation at Deming, New Mexico. Bob knew the area from El Paso to Yuma, which would become his primary backup route. He would continue to provide excellent service until I retired from pipeline patrol in 2010. We remain friends to this day.

Mooney versus Super Cub

Although nearly as old as Super Cub N82182, my 1962 Mooney M-20C and later my 1965 M-20E, were far superior in performance in the role of pipeline patrol. While the Cub struggled to make 85 mph, my Mooneys cruised easily at 120 mph using fewer gallons of fuel per hour. Additionally, as a four-place aircraft, they had much more interior space to store equipment, especially my cooler which sat on the cabin floor in front of the passenger's seat. Also, I could spread out my pipeline route charts on the front passenger's seat, making them easier to access. Safety-wise, the Mooneys gave me the capability to easily outrun burgeoning thunderstorms which, on occasion, nearly overtook the slower Cub.

Although the view of the ground was better from either side of the Cub's narrow fuselage, its high-wing configuration blocked out areas on the ground in a tight turn. I had no difficulty seeing the right of way through the left side of my Mooney's side windows by looking forward of the wing, although not everyone thought I could.

One morning while passing south of Stellar Air Park near Phoenix, a pilot in the landing pattern there asked on the VHF radio frequency how I could see the pipeline right of way from a low-wing aircraft. I replied, in all seriousness, that I had modified my left wing with a see-through Plexiglas section cut into the aluminum skin. He seemed amazed, noting that he'd never heard of such a thing, but accepted my word as fact. Fearing that he might spread an untrue story, I finally told him I was jesting, that there was no such modification and that I looked at the ground by looking ahead of the wing. He seemed disappointed.

A further advantage of my Mooney was that it was completely equipped for instrument flight and, as I was qualified to fly in instrument conditions, I could depart the California coast early in the day through low clouds which often moved in at night. I could also make instrument approaches when necessary. Additionally, my aircraft had two VHF radios, as opposed to the Cub's single radio, an immense help in heavy air traffic when I needed to monitor a second frequency.

Comparing patrol times, my Mooney could complete the entire route in 15 flight hours and one overnight stop, whereas it took 22 hours and two overnights in the Cub. The only downside to the

Mooney was that it was difficult to work on, as the engine was so tightly-cowled that even oil filter changes were tasks for smaller and more patient hands than mine. Also, parts for the airframe were harder to find and much more expensive.

Although I tried other types of patrol aircraft including Cessna, Citabria, Beechcraft, and Rockwell Commander, I never found one to equal my two Mooneys in speed and efficiency.

Winds and Weather

Pipeline patrol weather between San Diego and El Paso was not as cold as Calgary in winter nor as sizzling as the Sahara in summer, but it was harsh and changeable. Winter mornings in the high desert were often in the teens and summer temperatures exceeded 110 degrees. From early May until October, the best option was to be on patrol at first light and finish as early in the day as possible. During the coldest months, delaying my takeoff until after sunrise and using my cabin heater provided some relief from the icy blast of outside air.

Hot weather was a problem for my Mooney M-20E during 20-minute fuel stops, as the close-fitting engine cowling allowed heat to build up, which vaporized the fuel in the injector system. (The carbureted engine in my M-20C had no such problem and started easily in any weather). Hot starts in the M-20E were more of an art than a science, requiring adept manipulation of throttle, mixture control, and the auxiliary fuel pump. I found that a few choice words also helped during particularly balky starts.

Surface winds were a major factor, especially in the California mountain ranges and the passes where hurricane force winds were often experienced in fall and spring. On occasion, flying westbound through the Banning Pass west of Palm Springs, the turbulence was severe and my progress so slow that cars and trucks on Interstate 10 overtook me, a situation that they may have enjoyed, but I did not. The huge wind turbines in the Pass whirled like giant airplane propellers, an unnerving sight from several hundred feet above them and the surface winds raised clouds of dust difficult to see through.

Everywhere in the desert, from mid-morning until late afternoon, the heat produced hot air thermals of considerable violence. At my patrol speed of 120 mph, anything not securely tied down would careen about the cockpit, including my four toy ducks who accompanied me on every flight. I designated patrol segments on a basis of "one to four ducks," depending upon how many got airborne inside the cabin. A "four-ducker" was a rough ride indeed and I often wondered how long my elderly Mooneys could take such punishment, to say nothing of the pilot.

The haze and low clouds along the coastal portions of my route, from Los Angeles to San Diego, were often a problem, especially due to the commercial air traffic landing at the several fields along the coast. Under FAA tower control, I was cleared through their airspace on a not-to-interfere basis, which sometimes required me to make several orbits waiting for airliners to clear from my flight path.

During my 19 years of pipeline patrol, there were very few times I had to cancel a segment of my route due to severe weather conditions, such as exceptionally strong winds or winter snowstorms.

Chapter Thirteen
The Younger Pilot Generation

Patrolling my pipeline route near Hyder, Arizona, I scan the sky for F-16s from Luke Air Force Base which fly low-level training routes in my area and at my altitude. When I see them, in twos and often fours, I take delight in rolling in behind them and launching my imaginary Sidewinder missiles at their tailpipes. I have achieved "ace" status several times during my pipeline patrols, but I doubt the Air Force pilots from Luke even know it.

Strange how attitudes change with generations. Forty years ago, I would never have a allowed a civilian aircraft to make a run on my fighter. Up I'd pull, straight up, and roll over to reverse the tables on such an upstart, proving that the little mosquito had at least been sighted. No such reaction now. Maybe the pilots don't even see my small Mooney, busy as they are with their "computer game" cockpit displays. Maybe they don't care. Or, possibly, they fear they'll forfeit their pilot's wings if caught maneuvering against a civilian aircraft.

The poor devils will never know the freedom I knew as a young pilot. Flying from aircraft carriers in the Pacific, I often made low-level runs on fishing skiffs (and sometimes larger craft) lighting my afterburner as I passed 100 feet above them. In retrospect, however, I doubt that either the fishermen or the yachtsmen enjoyed my visits as much as I did.

Stateside, if we weren't satisfied with the number of flights we flew during the week, on weekends we could fly cross country "training flights" anywhere in the U.S., usually selecting air bases with the best happy hour bars and local entertainment.

These days, every pilot is required to file a flight plan for every flight and is closely monitored by Air Traffic Control. No more low-level flights viewing the landscape up close and personal. I'm sure today's fighter pilots would envy our weekly game of orbiting in the contrails over "enemy" bases, daring anyone to come up and engage in mock dogfights. There were always takers and we had some great battles, followed up whenever possible with friendly phone debriefs.

Suddenly, I spot two F-16s five miles away, just to the right of my aircraft's nose, about to cross my flight path. I rack my Mooney "fighter" up on a wing, checking to see if it's a flight of four. Sure enough, there is a second pair a mile behind the leader. In perfect position, I roll in behind number four as he passes one-half mile in front of my nose. Tracking "tail-end Charlie" with the blunt prop spinner on my fighter, I mash the imaginary firing button on my control wheel and shout to myself,

"Fox Two," certain of another Air Force kill.

The F-16s speed south, unaware of my Sidewinder missile's 160 pounds of steel and explosives closing in on their number four man. They make no defensive reaction at all. Satisfied, I roll back to my westerly heading, smiling my victory smile, certain that the F-16 flight leader will have difficulty explaining his return with only three aircraft, little suspecting that another Red Baron lives and hunts in a plane little faster than von Richthofen's World War I Fokker Tri-plane.

Seeing nothing but vultures and red tail hawks the rest of the way to Yuma, I call the tower for landing clearance ten miles northeast of the field, boosting my speed in hopes of arriving before an airliner inbound from 20 miles northwest. Looking at my airspeed indicator, stuck at 175 mph, I think back on my days in the F4 Phantom with its high-speed capability. No problem getting to Yuma ahead of the airliner in that machine. But that would have been long ago, and times have changed. How great it was to be a part of military aviation in the good old days.

The Deep Blue Sea

As I have related, I first sailed with my grandfather on the Hudson River at five years of age, already fascinated with the sea and ships of any kind. I loved the water world even more at the age of sixteen as I roared up and down the Hudson in a speedboat, often towing friends on water skis, day and night.

During my 1965-67 tour in USS Bon Homme Richard, I began racing small sailboats during our visits to Japan. The Japanese sailors, being small in stature, were tough to beat in light winds, but occasionally I'd get lucky.

Upon arriving at the Naval Postgraduate School in 1969, I started to take sailboat racing seriously, spending as much time as possible on Monterey Bay. By 1971, I was the Monterey Bay Yacht Club's champion in Shields-class sailboats.

During the late 1970s, I often chartered large sailboats in San Diego Bay and as far as the ultimate test of seamanship skills, I greatly enjoyed conning 75,000-ton USS Ranger in such evolutions as day and night underway replenishment operations, sometimes in heavy seas.

In 1983, while at Virginia Tech, I relished commanding the 43-foot sailboat assigned to my NROTC unit and in the late 1980s, I began chartering sailboats, and later, powerboats, in Washington State's San Juan Islands and the Canadian Gulf Islands.

Golden Wind

By 1999, Barbara and I were ready to expand our sailing horizons. In August, we joined several yachtsmen who agreed to purchase a 42-foot Catalina sailboat suitable for basing in the British Virgin Islands. As all members of the group were employed, the idea of time-sharing was attractive, particularly when it came to the considerable expense of not only purchasing the yacht but maintaining it.

I visited "Golden Wind" as she was being built at the Catalina yard in northeastern Los Angeles. She was a handsome sloop-rigged, three cabin model, which we deemed perfect for the Caribbean.

In January 2000, she was shipped by truck to St. Petersburg, Florida for final outfitting. I was to be captain for the first leg to Nassau, Bahamas via Key West. We had a crew of seven who were compatible and pleasant to sail with under the somewhat trying weather conditions during that time of year.

On our first leg to Key West, we encountered 25-knot northeast winds and 5-foot seas, a good shakedown for boat and crew. On the next leg to Nassau, crossing the Gulf Stream to the Grand Bahama Bank, wind speeds exceeded 35 knots with 8-foot seas. The most nerve-wracking part of the journey for me was the night approach to Nassau Harbor. Looking up in the dark, the whole crew gasped as our 59-foot mast barely cleared a bridge listed on the charts as 61 feet above the water.

For the next seven years, we enjoyed sailing Golden Wind in the British Virgin Islands. When she was finally returned to the States in 2007 and sold, all the partners had improved their sailing skills, enjoyed hosting family and friends, and agreed that it was one of the best experiences of our lives.

The British Virgin Islands

While sailing in the British Virgin Islands, we had ample time to observe the seamanship abilities of fellow yachtsmen, some skilled, some not. Many of the incidents were quite amusing, while others were a bit more serious, such as the events one evening at Trellis Bay on the north side of Beef Island.

As we had moored early in this prime location, our crew were enjoying rum "pain killers" while watching late-arriving sailboats negotiate the narrow channel into the bay. Right in front of us, one sailboat about 32 feet in length, with the captain at the wheel and his female first mate standing on the foredeck, boathook in hand, fetched up hard on an underwater rock with a tremendous boom, which to me sounded as if a large metal dumpster had been dropped 20 feet onto a concrete driveway. The sailboat decelerated from five knots to zero in about two feet, pitching the foredeck crew flat on her face, boathook and all. Unhurt physically, but fractured emotionally, she scrambled to her feet and directed a stream of invective at her careless captain, who in return muttered something about "unreliable charts." Backing up a few feet and still afloat, the captain eased back into the channel, and proceeded to a nearby mooring buoy for the night.

Shaking my head, I remarked to our crew that witnessing such an event was quite rare and a good learning experience. Yet, not five minutes later, the event proved less rare as an identically sized boat, with a duplicate crew of two, fetched up on the same rock with the same result, namely a loud boom and a prostrate female crewmember on the foredeck clutching her boathook. She, too, was unhurt and directed equally abusive language at her surprised captain who, in all likelihood, was also the victim of faulty charts. Visibly chagrined, the captain backed off the rock, regained the channel, and proceeded to a buoy next to the first boat. Possibly they were friends, rather used to doing things together.

The next morning, both boats were still afloat, however, my bet was that the charter company owning the boats found significant hull damage when the boats returned to port.

Willy Thornton

Anchored in Norman Island Bay, was a large, old, former workboat called the "Willy Thornton," well known for its rowdy bar and a stern platform some ten feet above the water from which nubile damsels were encouraged to jump off topless, the reward being a free drink, a round of appreciative applause (louder for some than others), and a T-shirt stenciled, "I jumped topless off the Willy Thornton!"

My wife, Barbara, being somewhat Victorian, let it be known that any female member of our crew who participated in such an event would have to book passage back to port on another boat. Barbara's rather nubile cousin, Debbie, was disappointed, as were several of our male crewmembers. I, of course, agreed with Barbara.

A Broken Alternator Belt

While Golden Wind had few maintenance problems, we did experience one approaching Jost Van Dyke Island, home of "Foxy's," the bar featuring many ladies' undergarments hanging from the rafters above the food and drink.

In late October 2004, on the approach to the harbor entrance under engine power, the alternator belt snapped, stopping the engine cooling pump, which resulted in an immediate engine overheat warning light. Abandoning the approach, we set sail for the return to our home port of Nanny Cay on Tortola Island.

Radioing ahead, we were met at the harbor entrance by "Stick," newly hired by our maintenance manager. Stick was bundled up against the 85-degree chill in a full-length ski jacket and hunkered down in a 12-foot dingy with a line suitable to tow an ocean liner into port. Nicknamed for his physical (and we suspect mental) resemblance to a twig, Stick appeared to be in a bit of a funk, having been called away from his morning regimen of breakfast burritos and beer, the aroma of both items quite noticeable on his breath.

Eventually making it to the pier, and upon viewing our onboard spare belt, Stick opined that it was far too small, whereupon he headed down the pier for the large-belt locker, which happened to be adjacent to the bar.

Some 45 minutes later, Stick reappeared with an even stronger aroma of beer and a belt that would encircle the entire vessel, proudly announcing that, "this puppy will sure fit." He was somewhat taken aback to find that during his lengthy absence I had installed the "too small" belt and we were ready for sea. Swearing we would not divulge the details of the repair job to his boss, thus ruining his reputation as a top mechanic, Stick headed back to the bar for lunch.

Stick, incidentally, was usually assisted by Caroline, also a new hire, who was as lean as he was but, upon first impression, appeared to be at least a half-step ahead of him in the smarts department. First impressions, however, are not always accurate, as Caroline had a fetish for ascending 60-foot masts in a bosun's chair, reportedly being the only one in the marina who would do so willingly at no extra pay.

Returning to sea, we made it to Jost late in the day to be greeted by swarms of mosquitoes which were also an annoyance to the locals, based upon the rhythmic sounds of hands swatting naked flesh coming from the various shops and porches along the only street in town. The on-duty matron at the combined Customs House and Police Station paused from her deterrent efforts long enough to note that "the buggers get really bad after sunset."

We didn't wait to find out, making for nearby Sopers Hole on the western end of Tortola in a driving rainstorm. Along with two other sailboats in the channel, we were serenaded by the ship's horn on the "Bomba Express," the inter-island seagoing bus, incensed that lesser vessels were in "his channel." Moored to the only remaining buoy in the harbor, we gladly repaired below decks and out of the rain for rum pain killers. The mosquitoes, we think, remained at Jost.

Investments

Of the ways to increase one's net worth, I have found investing in real estate to be the only reliable method. Since purchasing our first house in San Diego in 1957, we have bought sixteen properties, thirteen in California, and one each in Texas, Colorado, and New Mexico, three of which remain in our possession. By far, the best investments have been in the Golden State.

While I'm normally a careful buyer, in mid-2000 there was a notable exception…Randsburg, California. My right ankle was in a cast at the time, the result of mishandling my 800-pound motorcycle, which I claim influenced my judgement in plunking down $15,000 for a place in the desert, sight unseen.

A close family friend who was also a real estate broker mentioned one day that she had spotted an exceptional deal in the quaint town of Randsburg, a place frequented by rock-hounds and bikers on their way to other desert locations.

"Except when one's ears are under assault from noisy dirt bikes," she claimed, "it's possible to hear the muffled flapping of birds' wings flying low overhead and it's a nearly perfect place to find relief from busy city life. And how can you go wrong on a two-bedroom house for $15,000?" We were about to find out.

Researching, I found that Randsburg is in the Mojave Desert about 60 miles east of Bakersfield. As the area experiences little rainfall, the town, other than a few buildings, consists largely of sand and various species of cactus. There are limited overnight accommodations and any chance for a meal ceases at sundown.

The two bright spots we found were Charlie's Ore Shop, a hot spot to pick up bargain rocks, etc., and a bar called "The Joint," which we found to be a handy place to get a two-dollar warm beer or even a martini, provided you brought your own olives and vermouth. The owner, Olga, who appeared to have been a redhead once upon a time, claimed to have known the Mercury astronauts on a first name basis. As she was getting along in years, by now the establishment may have a new owner.

A major attraction for me was that my all-time movie hero, Robert Duvall, of "Lonesome Dove" fame, regularly visited a friend of his in town, which meant I might have a chance to chat with good old Augustus McCrae.

The structure of interest to us, 333 Highland Avenue, was located 200 feet upslope from The Joint, which, while an easy trip down for refreshments, was a bit more taxing on the way home in the dark, especially considering the risk of encountering rattlesnakes, scorpions, and other night-loving creatures.

I was delighted, although Barbara was not, to find that our ghost town fixer could be had at such a reasonable price, hardly what an upscale doghouse costs in the southern part of the state. While the two-bedroom, one-bath structure did have a few imperfections, such as several "observation ports" in the roof and an unlocatable septic system, which I suspected emptied into the Yellow Aster Gold mine directly beneath the bathroom, I thought it would be an ideal getaway. I was wrong.

Making all kinds of high-priced concessions to Barbara, I finally convinced her to spend one night there sleeping on cots and eating from a picnic cooler. As it was not raining, things went reasonably well until about midnight, when a spider or scorpion, we couldn't tell which in the dark, dropped onto Barbara's cot. That did it. If I wanted to overnight there ever again it would be solo, she informed me, and no enticement could change her mind...period!

The next morning on the way out of town, we stopped by Charlie's. While there, I mentioned to Clara, the shop's manager and former owner of 333 Highland Ave., that, sadly, we were putting it back on the market. Looking up from his morning coffee, an elderly gentleman seated nearby, interrupted saying loudly,

"I'll buy it."

Stunned and thinking I'd misheard, I turned and introduced myself as the proud owner. The gentleman shook my hand and introduced himself as Ben Thompson, long-time resident and part-time gold miner.

"Ben," I asked, "are you sure you know which house I'm talking about?"

Ben allowed that he was very familiar with the place, often having gazed up at it as he was departing The Joint at sunset. In reply to my confession that the roof had a few holes, he noted that,

"It's not much of a problem as it doesn't rain much here."

Still trying to convince him that it might not be a good investment, Ben cheerfully countered every point I brought up. Warming to the prospect that he indeed might buy the place and worried that our only other option might be a pro bono lease to a local Boy Scout troop as a tax write-off, I grandly offered it to Ben for a mere $16,000, with small monthly payments after a substantial down payment. Clara, who knew Ben well, informed me that he was most reliable and that he received a monthly World War II Army pension which she helped him manage. Not only that, but Clara offered to cosign a note for the full amount.

By this time, Barbara had ceased glaring at me and her frown had given way to a smile. Things were improving on the home front.

As Ben declined my offer to let him inspect the property, the deal was closed on the spot. I handed him the keys, truthfully noting that only one door had a lock, to which he replied,

"I never lock my doors anyway."

It was the quickest and easiest real estate transaction I had ever made. Never mind the minimum profit. Besides, it appeared that Barbara once again regarded me as a genius…at least in extracting myself from such a perilous situation.

Departing southbound, Barbara joined me in wondering how we had gotten so lucky, so quickly. Then a disquieting thought crossed my mind…did Ben know something I didn't? Was the Yellow Aster about to make the owner a lucrative deal just to cease flooding the mine from his bathroom's toilet?

As it turned out, however, the Yellow Aster was not involved. Ben was just plain tired of living in his trailer and wanted a house close to town, and maybe The Joint, so he didn't have to walk so far in the dark. Unfortunately, he got to enjoy his new digs for only five years.

In December 2006, we received a check in the mail from Clara for the full amount owed by Ben and a note informing us that Ben had gone to the "big gold mine in the sky." As the new owner, she would fix a few remaining flaws and keep it as a family guest house. Given the eight-hour roundtrip, we never returned to Randsburg to see how it turned out.

Pets and Other Animals

Like many families, mine always had in residence several dogs and often a cat or two. At our Walden, N.Y. home, we also had two, sometimes three horses, a milk cow, chickens, and occasionally, pigs.

One exotic addition was a young red fox named "Reddy." He was always up to some caper including stalking our chickens and, now and again, escaping from his large enclosure. I took him for long walks in nearby fields and woods at the end of a leash hooked to a dog harness. Reddy had been given to us by a neighbor who rescued him and his several siblings from a den after their parents had been killed by hunters.

While hardly snuggly or affectionate, he was not in the least ill-tempered or aggressive towards humans. Reddy came to grief when he escaped his enclosure one afternoon and was shot by a farmer, convinced Reddy was a wild fox stalking the farmer's chickens.

While we had a few small dogs, we tended to favor large ones, such as "Viking," a 120-pound, fawn-colored Great Dane strong enough to support my 60-pound body on his back. Viking was romantically interested in my uncle's female Irish Wolfhound and during certain times of the year would happily drag my brother and me in a small wagon hooked to his choke collar over the one-mile trip in record time.

The problem was getting him back, so we usually ended up by putting him in our wagon and towing *him* home. While not aggressive toward humans, Viking and his running mate, a female fox hound named "Brownie," took up the forbidden sport of harassing the neighbors' sheep, which ended badly for them both, at the hands of angry farmers.

Of the more than twenty canines we've known over the years, the most unusual was a wolf hybrid we called "Luke." I include here my tribute to him after his passing in 2004.

Chapter Fourteen
Tribute to a Wolf

Luke

15 July 1991-24 January 2004

He came to us in the fall of 1991, a rather scraggly, eight-week-old specimen of his tribe, angular and all ears, the gift of our future daughter-in-law, Chris, anxious to curry favor with us and our son, her beloved macho man, Jason.

His mother was a full-blooded wolf, his dad half-wolf, half-Malamute. We named him "Luke." The first I learned of his presence was when I called Barbara from a Phoenix phone booth at the end of my day bouncing low over the desert on my weekly pipeline patrol.

"Luke will be here only a little while," she said. "Chris and Jason will take him away when they have a home of their own."

I wasn't sure when that would be.

We immediately found that Luke was different from any animal we have ever owned, or should I say, shared food and shelter with. Mischievous, sly, quick to take advantage of an open gate or a fence less than six feet high, keeping track of him was a constant challenge. Late at night, he would sometimes escape and roam the neighborhood. We could determine his general location by listening to our neighbors' dogs sounding off as he made his rounds.

Luke's specialties were cats and stray chickens. Whichever he could sink his two-inch incisors into first, became his catch of the day. Luke wasn't mean or vicious, he was just being a wolf and wolves capture prey, no matter the owner. By morning, Luke would always return home, having somehow eluded speeding cars and irate neighbors sweeping chicken feathers and cat's fur off their lawns.

At first, we mounted search parties, combing every street and alley within miles, but Luke was never to be seen, for at night he was nearly invisible. During our evening walks, I marveled at how in the gathering dusk and just a few feet away from me, he could melt into the background. I had never known a creature of that size, some 90 pounds, who could disappear before my eyes.

At age two, Luke was a magnificent sight, cloaked in a long, luxuriant coat of iron-gray with black-rimmed amber eyes, and a large head filled with teeth rivaling those of a male African lion. Lesser animals gave him a wide berth. Shy with people, but fiercely territorial, Luke would not hesitate to attack dogs twice his size. While sometimes outgunned in sheer strength, his quickness always befuddled his adversaries.

His one nemesis was a huge, ugly critter, half pit bull and half Great Dane, a bête noire who would certainly have wreaked havoc were he to catch Luke. Luke, however, would make a mockery of his bumbling charges, darting left and right until his foe flopped down exhausted, hoping in vain that Luke would also tire. But Luke was a wolf and wolves, we found, never tire.

Luke loved to ride in the back of our truck, head out of the camper shell window, enjoying the breeze and the scenery. He favored the right rear window closest to the sidewalk, which caused many a stare from curious pedestrians. Luke was not good with children who, for some reason, always wanted to touch the one animal we suggested they not touch.

When annoyed, Luke's deep, throaty growl and quick head movement with bared teeth towards the source of his irritation, invariably caused child and beast to back off. Despite his fearsome appearance and actions, Luke never touched teeth to human flesh, but we were always acutely aware that he was not far removed from the wild and was equipped to do great damage.

With other animals, particularly male dogs, it was a different story. Although a ferocious fighter, Luke was interested in domination, not destruction. As soon as his foe gave up, Luke welcomed him into the "wolfpack."

While Luke had a keen sense of smell, he was primarily a sight hunter. During our runs together through fields of brush, I would try to hide, but he always found me. Teaming up with "Sienna," our golden retriever, who invariably picked up my scent, Luke followed her until he spied me. It was an unsettling experience to be hunkered down behind a bush and hear their thundering footsteps approaching. When Luke finally burst upon me, his toothy, glowering face a few feet from me, I can imagine how our cave-dwelling ancestors may have felt when faced with such a creature.

In his later years, Luke mellowed. By the time he was eight, he seemed less interested in territory and more interested in the ladies, a sure sign of maturity. His one great love was a pretty, blue-eyed Husky named Xenia, after the warrior princess, I think. They would dash about during our evening walks, Xenia blinded by his good looks and Luke enthralled with Xenia's future possibilities. To our relief and probably to Luke's dismay, Xenia was treated to a visit with a vet before things got too far along. We often wondered how their offspring would have looked and acted.

In the last year of his life, Luke became more restrained in his behavior. Maybe he had a touch of arthritis or had lived too full a life. Every night as I sat in my large leather chair, Luke would come to me and insist upon being petted. Only then would he retire to the other side of the room to sleep. No matter where in the house he was, I knew that if I sat in my chair for five minutes he would be there. And he always was.

Luke is gone, victim of a brain tumor. Yet, up to the last day of his life, he insisted on his daily walk, so important for dogs and more so for a wolf. Since his passing, not a day goes by without me remembering our 13 years together and my privilege of communing with a special animal one generation removed from the wild. Indeed, when Luke was young, there were times I feared he might revert to being wild. He was often restless and sometimes difficult to control.

If he focused on an animal across a field, his mind blocked out my commands and, if not leashed, he would dash off to investigate. Extremely social to the point of barely tolerating being left alone, he taxed our patience regularly. Yet, when we looked into his bright eyes, stroked his magnificent coat and watched him run across an open field, a picture of strength, grace, and beauty, our family knew that he was God's special gift to us.

I have talked with pastors, philosophers, and others who have a deep and abiding faith in the Almighty. Often, they have differing ideas of what constitutes the Hereafter. Some claim that only "beings" with "souls," and the ability to reason will ascend to Heaven.

I take issue with that. For me, I cannot accept that Heaven can be a pleasant place to spend eternity without the faithful and loving pets who have shared our lives. Should I rate ascendance to that Place, I am convinced that all the pets I've known will be there and that Luke will be the first to greet me.

Our family has been touched by a wolf and we are the better for it. Rest well, dear Luke….

The End of an Era

I flew for the first time in June 1948 in my father's new Ercoupe, a two-place, 75-horsepower light plane capable of speeds of nearly 100 miles an hour. Dad had soloed in a J-3 Piper Cub the month prior, from a small airport called Freedom Plains in upstate New York. Along with his instructor, I observed his first solo landings and take offs, all of them precisely executed. The only sign of his nervousness appeared to be a long-stemmed piece of grass he was chewing on that became shorter each circuit of the field. Shortly thereafter, dad was awarded his private pilot's license which allowed him to take passengers with him, day or night.

In late 1948, tired of the Ercoupe's limited capabilities, dad traded it for a North American Aviation Navion, a four-place, 185-horsepower aircraft, which could fly from New York to Florida in one day. Although still too young to solo, I learned how to fly, navigate, and maintain a complex airplane.

Continuing my interest in aviation, in 1954 I embarked on my 30-year career as a naval aviator, accumulating over 6000 flight hours in dozens of different aircraft, including the best fighter and attack aircraft of the day. I'm proud to note that, other than minor damage to my FJ-3 in 1958 after a total engine failure at 200 feet altitude, my most serious incident was a flat tire caused by running over a nail during my taxi to a runway for takeoff in a TF-10B.

My good record continued in civilian life. From 1985 to 2015, I flew many types of light aircraft and sailplanes, highlighted by over 10,000 flight hours of pipeline patrol, again with no damage other than a dent in one wing of my patrol aircraft caused by a territorial, or possibly suicidal, hawk. The dent was easily repaired, the hawk was not.

By 1998 I had worn out my first Mooney which was at a point where major structural repairs were needed, namely the replacement of the center section of the wings which showed considerable corrosion.

In February, I bought another Mooney, a 1965 M20E, featuring a fuel-injected 200-horsepower Lycoming engine and a dazzling, highly polished aluminum exterior. N65GL never failed to evoke favorable comments everywhere I flew.

In my final years of pipeline patrol, I vividly recall the pleasure of departing El Paso International airport just before sunrise, when the high clouds in the eastern sky were tinted pink. Passing over brightly lighted downtown El Paso, my Lycoming engine seemed always to run more smoothly in the cool morning air.

Westbound, my polished silver wings reflected the pink clouds, a most peaceful and inspiring sight. In the cabin, my four toy ducks rested comfortably, ready for the thrashing they would take as the morning thermals began.

Flying low, approaching my first fuel stop at Deming, New Mexico, I could peer into the nests of red tail hawks, built on the cross members of power poles. Below, beef cattle grazed among small herds of antelopes and packs of coyotes often gave me a ringside seat to their coordinated hunting efforts.

On 26 January 2010, in the best pipeline patrol flying weather I had yet experienced, I flew my last patrol. Although cold, there were no surface winds anywhere along my route, from San Diego to El Paso. In over 1700 crossings of the high desert, this trip was the most pleasant…very fitting for my final patrol.

Faced with the high cost of maintaining a private airplane without the benefits of using it as a business, in July 2011 I sold N65GL to an engineer at Cape Kennedy, Florida. He and his young family were pleased to have such a fine-looking airplane with such a unique history. I'm glad my Mooney will continue to fly.

Not ready to quit flying, I entered into a partnership with a friend who owned a Cessna 150, a nicely equipped aircraft in excellent condition. However, despite sharing costs, the all-inclusive price of an hour's flight time was nearly $100 which, when flying at a speed little more than that of a car, became less attractive each month. On 13 September 2013, I flew my last flight in a powered aircraft.

I did stay proficient in sailplanes, however, flying in Florida during the winter and in New York State in summer. While less expensive than powered flight, it was fun only for me, as Barbara preferred not to be onboard while I flew aimlessly, she claimed, in circles, alongside hawks and vultures.

On 27 September 2015, at Middletown, New York, not far from where I first took to the air in 1948, I flew my last flight in N17924, a single-seat Schweitzer I-26E, one of the oldest sailplanes of its kind still operational. While I didn't know it at the time, it was my last flight as pilot in command.

Do I miss flying? In certain regards I do, as I've always enjoyed the freedom of the skies. Now, though, the FAA imposes strict control over all but the most remote airspace. Most of all, I'll miss the convenience of flying about the country in my own plane at a time of my choosing, avoiding security lines in crowded terminals and the cattle drives known as boarding and deplaning.

Aviation has been a way of life for me for nearly three-quarters of a century and I often reminisce with friends about the joys and challenges of that unique profession. Most significantly, I'll always be pleased that over the many years and thousands of flights, my takeoffs and landings remain exactly equal in number.

My years at sea, from 1938 until 2007, were a most special and pleasurable time for me, my family and friends. The oceans have been good to me and, despite what my submariner friends might say, I'm happy to report that I've always remained on top, rather than under the water. I'm equally pleased to note that I always returned to port with an undamaged craft and with the same number of crew members that I began with. Looking back, it was a long, happy era for me.

Barbara
Maple Bay, Canada
June 1991

George and Steve Waggoner
Canadian Gulf Islands
June 1991

Philip and Alexa
Encinitas, California
July 2016

The Condon Family
L-R Dennis, Jennifer, Kathy, Victoria
Encinitas, California
July 2007

Alexa Condon
Encinitas, California
November 2019

Jason and Chris VandeWater
Encinitas, California
May 2011

John Falvella, George
Barbara, Bette Falvella
Ukraine River Boat
"Lomonosov"
October 2013

George and Barbara
British Virgin Islands
November 2006

Chapter Fifteen
My Greatest Loss

Barbara Gay VandeWater
19 December 1936-12 May 2018

On 12 May 2018, after over 62 years of marriage, I lost Barbara to lung cancer. She had begun smoking at the age of 15, not an unusual habit for teenagers anxious to mimic movie stars and high-profile personalities. However, in the fall of 1984, her two-pack-a day habit stopped abruptly during an emotional phone call from our nurse daughter, Kathy, who relayed the words of a patient dying of lung cancer. "If you love someone who smokes," the woman pleaded, "please convince them to stop."

"Mom," Kathy said, "she looked just like you and had three children gathered at her bedside." That did it. Barbara stopped smoking…cold turkey. But during 32 years of smoking, the damage had been done.

I wrote this letter to our friends informing them of her passing:

6/20/18

Dear Friends,

It is with profound sadness and a sense of irreplaceable loss that I must tell you our Barbara died on 12 May 2018. For some years, she had suffered from back and leg problems which she overcame with sheer grit. In February 2017, she experienced a minor stroke, from which she was recovering, when in early 2018 she was diagnosed with lung cancer, followed rapidly by spine cancer. In late April, she was hospitalized in extreme pain which could not be controlled by medication and she went rapidly downhill. While her bruised and battered body was emaciated, her face remained serenely beautiful. Our entire family and our pastor were at her bedside at the end. Services were held on Saturday, 9 June and she was inurned at Miramar National Cemetery on Friday, 15 June 2018.

As you know, Barbara and I had a remarkable 62 years of marriage during which we did many things that some can only dream of. With the support of our three children, Jason, Kathy, and Philip and our close friends, I'm doing as best I can, although the enormity of our loss has yet to sink in.

After some 50 years of my Christmas letters, poking fun at world events and even family and friends, I think this note will have to suffice for 2018. I know Barbie would join me in thanking each of you for the wonderful memories we've shared over many years. Thanks for being our very dear friends. I am certain that we shall all meet again someday.

Love to all,
George

A Lasting Attraction

As a tribute to Barbara, in August 2018 I presented this summary of our life together at a writers' class I regularly attend:

In my first eighteen years of life, Barbara was not the first pretty girl I had become infatuated with...but she was the last. Of medium height and well proportioned, she had beautiful brown hair and the piercing hazel eyes of her paternal Prussian ancestors. When Barbara gazed at me, I felt she was looking directly into my soul.

From her mother, she had inherited the nearly flawless skin of British women, tinted tan by the summer sun and a pert, well-formed nose that women pay plastic surgeons to acquire.

As a counterpoint to my overly jocular demeanor, Barbara was somewhat reserved, waiting it seemed, for me to make the first mistake. I had never met anyone like her. I was enthralled.

Not one to make snap judgments, on the 26th day of August 1952, I did just that. I made up my mind that if she would have me, I wanted her to be my life's companion. Initially unimpressed by my country boy background and brash persona, I slowly worked my way into her confidence, partly with toys that appealed to a city girl, but also with my sincere efforts to convince her I'd be a good and proper husband. It took me three years to do so.

We began married life in January 1956 in a small cottage in Coronado, California. While I flew Navy airplanes from nearby NAS North Island and had fun, she tended to the household and what would become, over the years, a family of three children. At age 19, she was the youngest of the 22 wives in our first squadron. Fascinated with the stories the older women told about the exotic lands they had visited and the excitement of Navy life, Barbara was convinced that she could never again be content in a town like Newburgh, N.Y.

During our 30-year Navy career, we were stationed at numerous West Coast naval air stations and spent three years at the beautiful Naval Postgraduate School in Monterey, California. During my carrier-based deployments to the Pacific, Barbara met me in Hong Kong and the Philippine Islands, seeing first-hand how the Asians lived.

During our four-year tour in Thailand, Barbara traveled with me throughout Southeast Asia. As I was the U.S. Naval Attaché to Thailand, Burma, and Laos, we often attended as many as five diplomatic parties in one evening. Barbara never tired, enjoying every moment. She related especially well to the twenty-six members of the Military Attaché Corps of Thailand and their wives.

Equally at ease with royalty and diplomats as she was with street vendors and our household help, everyone loved Barbara.

In retirement, we continued to travel. For twenty-five years, we flew our small airplane to forty-five of the fifty states and for seven years based our sailboat in the British Virgin Islands. We made river boat cruises to Russia, France, Portugal, and Ukraine and rode trains throughout Europe.

Of Barbara's many qualities, foremost of which was her kind and loving nature, there was also a hint of quiet determination in achieving her family-oriented goals. While I ricocheted from one unachievable project to the next, she focused on the doable. If Barbara made up her mind to do it, it would be done…one way or the other. And in the end, despite my occasional foot-dragging, I'd be as pleased about the way things turned out as she was.

I believe most of us have lived lives which, save for a chapter or two, we would not change. I feel likewise. My life with Barbara was happy, eventful, rewarding, and just plain fun. We did things and lived lifestyles enjoyed by few others. Carved in marble on our niche at Miramar National Cemetery are the words suggested by our son, Jason, which I feel are the very essence of our 62 years together:

LET IT BE KNOWN…WE LIVED

Adrift

As a nautical term, adrift means "underway" with no way on. In other words, neither moored nor anchored, drifting through the water with no means of propulsion, at the mercy of wind and current, unable to steer for a destination.

Kathleen Gay VandeWater Condon
18 January 1959-10 March 2019

Since Barbara's passing in May 2018, I have been adrift, a situation made worse by the loss of our daughter, Kathy, in March 2019, also to lung cancer. Kathy spent her entire adult life as a Registered Nurse, attending to infants at a Kaiser Permanente Hospital in the Los Angeles area. She leaves behind her husband Dennis, two daughters, Victoria and Jennifer, and a granddaughter, Alexa. Kathy was only 60 years of age.

I now spend nearly all my time at home, with little desire to travel or even visit places close by. A large portrait of Barbara hangs over our fireplace, looking down. She has a slight "Mona Lisa" smile which in dim lighting I swear I can see her lips moving, silently mouthing to me "I love you." Although my mind knows better, my heart wishes to believe she is on one of the shopping trips she so loved and that she'll soon return. I am surrounded by memorabilia and pictures of us together. All her clothes, cosmetics, and everyday items are still in place, untouched.

The last U.S. flag flown over our sailboat, Golden Wind, hangs in my office, along with the cocktail pennant we have sailed with on several boats since 1984. The pennant is inscribed with cruise dates, boat names, and crewmembers.

The last date is July 2007, listing our crew of Tom and Cathy Valenzia and our son-in-law, Dennis, on our voyage from Charleston, South Carolina to Annapolis, Maryland where Golden Wind was put up for sale. During our years of shared ownership with several friends, I take pride in having been captain on her first voyage in February 2000 and on her last voyage in July 2007, accompanied as always by my First Mate, Barbara.

Our sons, Jason and Philip, live close by and, along with Jason's wife, Chris, are of great comfort to me. Our small dog, Maggie, which Barbara so loved, is my constant companion. While Maggie seems happy, I note she takes great interest in any woman she sees, hoping I think, that one will turn out to be her long-lost mother…Barbara.

One of my favorite photos of Barbara was taken in June 1991 during our cruise in the Canadian Gulf Islands aboard the sailboat, "Mere Belle." Barbara is in the bloom of perfect health, her face and hair as beautiful as the Canadian scenery. She is at the helm, steering the boat and enjoying the brisk weather, along with our friends, Greta and Steve Waggoner.

While the Canadian Gulf Islands offer good cruising, at least in the summer months, our favorite cruising destination has been the British Virgin Islands where the warm waters teem with fish, easily viewed through a snorkel mask. Barbara was an excellent swimmer and spent many happy hours in those pristine waters.

Maybe I'll opt for a quiet cabin in the woods for a few weeks each year, where I'll have more animal than human neighbors. City life has its conveniences, but also its drawbacks. Having spent my formative years on a farm, I much prefer the open spaces. Had I lived 150 years ago, I'm certain I would have signed on with a wagon train, just for a look at what was beyond the far horizon.

In Retrospect

In reviewing my life's story, I fear that the last few chapters have cast a somewhat somber note on what otherwise has been a happy and eventful life. In fact, others have experienced even more severe losses than have I. They have survived and flourished and so will I.

I sometimes wonder what I would have become had I not spent 30 years as a naval aviator. My high school peers, for the most part, remained close to where they grew up, taking over a family business or becoming professionals or bureaucrats. Maybe I'd have been a salesman or, heaven forbid, a politician.

Now that the hometown friends I grew up with have all passed from the scene and, except to pay my respects to my dad, brother, and close relatives buried in the area, I no longer feel the need to visit the place where I spent my first 20 years. Visiting my mom, who is buried with my stepfather at Fort Bliss National Cemetery in El Paso, is a shorter trip which I often make.

Although my paternal and maternal ancestors have lived in the Northeast since the early 1600s, beginning in 1955, I have called California home. While the Golden State teems with cars and people, my street is quiet and peaceful. Neighbors are friendly but not overwhelming and I see the Pacific Ocean every day. Looking westward, I relish the memories of the personal and professional experiences I've had in the Pacific, either in a warship or ashore in interesting and very different lands.

While I'm intensely proud of my 30-year career in what I feel is the finest branch of our military services, when I retired, I shifted gears. While I don't criticize others for doing so, I don't wear a military-themed cap or jacket emblazoned with patches depicting the many units I was part of. I haven't visited an officers' club bar since 1985, the year I retired. For whom among the young aviators of today, enthralled with their video game cockpits, would care to listen to an elderly flyer speak of the old days before computers flew airplanes? Yet, when asked or when the subject comes up in conversation, I will expound at length upon the virtues of the Navy, especially naval aviation. And I speak with reverence of the squadron mates I flew with over the many years.

All my life, I have been active, hyperactive, some say. I find it difficult to relax, as so many others can. Fortunately, I have no physical restrictions and I exercise regularly. My mind remains clear and I can recall events and conversations as far back as my third year of life, an immense help in writing my story.

And now that my story is up to date, I intend to shift my efforts to editing some 50 years of my Christmas letters which cover each year's events in a humorous light, poking fun at events, family, friends…and even myself. Some letters extend to several pages with photos and press excerpts to make my point. Best of all, it will give me something to do, until there's more to write in my life's story.

Epilogue

Over the course of my story I have not mentioned family and friends as much as I might have. Perhaps the following may help.

Barbara and I brought three children into the world: eldest son, Jason Loft, born 30 March 1957 at the Naval Hospital Annex in Coronado, California; daughter, Kathleen Gay (Kathy as we called her) born 18 January 1959 in Alameda, California; youngest son, Philip Edwin, born 14 February 1964 in Escondido, California.

All three were with us at our various duty stations until September 1976. While Jason remained in Encinitas, Kathy and Philip accompanied us to Thailand. Both Kathy and Philip graduated high school at the International School of Bangkok. Kathy departed for Encinitas after graduation while Philip remained with us.

During his four years in Thailand, Philip learned the Thai language quickly and remains reasonably fluent in speaking this difficult language. He often spent time in the countryside with his Thai friends.

From the age of 18 onward Jason has been involved in the construction business, first as a laborer and finally as a master carpenter. As an active, licensed contractor he has designed, renovated, and built numerous houses in Texas and California. Jason had two sons by his first wife, Leslie. He has been married to his second wife, Christin, since 1996. They have no children, opting instead for a procession of pets, including horses and dogs. They live next door to me in Encinitas.

Kathy graduated San Diego State University in 1986 with a Bachelor of Science degree in nursing. She spent her adult life as a Registered Nurse in Kaiser hospitals in the Los Angeles area until her death in March 2019 from lung cancer. She had a short marriage to her first husband, Howard Doerfling. Their daughter, Victoria, lives in the San Diego area. Kathy and her second husband, Dennis Condon, have a daughter, Jennifer.

Philip learned to play guitar in Bangkok and attended the Guitar Institute of Technology in Los Angeles. All his life he has played in various bands and composed songs. He lives in Encinitas and remains unmarried with no entangling alliances.

Barbara's sister, Bette Jane, and her husband, John Falvella, live in Rock Tavern, New York. Over the years we have become very close, sailing together in the Caribbean and traveling on river boats in Europe, Russia, and Ukraine.

I have no living relatives in my hometown of Newburgh, New York. The friends I grew up with have passed on. I occasionally visit to pay my respects to my brother and my father who are buried in Walden, New York and to visit family friends.

There remain alive two of my cousins. Mary Jane D'Arrigo, the daughter of my uncle Legrand, lives in Irvington, New York. Ellen Chadwick Arbogast, the daughter of my aunt Francis, lives in Orlando, Florida. I see then rarely.

My dad died in May 1961 in Middletown, New York at age 55, the victim of heart disease. Mom died in April 1998 in El Paso, Texas at the age of 85. She was vigorous until she suffered a fatal stroke.

I have one grandson, Justin Telles, two granddaughters, Victoria Doerfling and Jennifer Condon, and a great granddaughter, Alexa Condon.

One of my earliest friendships was with Leo Carmody, who introduced me to Barbara in 1952. Leo died in February 1998 in Naples Florida from cancer.

Cdr. Bob Nave, who was instrumental in my decision to make the Navy my career, died in December 2002 in Houston, Texas of natural causes.

My NavCad 4-54 classmate, Harvey Taylor and his wife, Betty, live in Nicolaus, California. Although we talk by phone, I have not seen them since October 2003.

Donna and Bill Ball
Coronado, California
June 2003

Marine colonel, Bill Ball, died in November 2014 in San Diego, California after a long bout with Parkinson's disease. His wife, Donna, whom I see occasionally, lives in Coronado, California.

Lcdr. John Hamilton, of Key West fame, whereabouts are unknown. I last saw him in March 1963. He would be in his late 90s if he were still alive.

My squadron mate, Captain Ron Johnson and his wife, Mary, live in Santa Maria, California. I see them occasionally.

Another squadron mate, Dave Dungan and his wife, Jan, live in Salt Lake City, Utah. I see them occasionally.

Captain John Nicholson, former commanding officer USS Ranger and his wife, Evelyn, live in Santa Maria, California. I saw "Nick" in September 2019 during a talk he gave at NAS Lemoore, California about his participation in the "Tonkin Gulf" incident which turned out to be the beginning of the Vietnam war.

Longtime friends, Steve and Greta Waggoner, live in Escondido, California. I see them frequently.

Aviation and sailing friends, Tom and Cathy Valenzia, have homes in Escondido, California and Charleston, South Carolina. I see them occasionally.

George L. VandeWater

Author
George L. VandeWater
And
Mooney Aircraft

www.ingramcontent.com/pod-product-compliance
Lightning Source LLC
LaVergne TN
LVHW091547060526
838200LV00036B/742